Charles Wassermann's more than 4000 mile-long journey through the german territories under polish administration, took him from the east prussian-russian frontier through Danzig and the former Polish Corridor to Pomerania, East Brandenburg and Silesia.

EUROPE'S FORGOTTEN
TERRITORIES

CHARLES WASSERMANN

EUROPE'S FORGOTTEN TERRITORIES

1960

R. ROUSSELL COPENHAGEN

This book first appeared in Germany under the title:
"Unter Polnischer Verwaltung", and was published by
Blüchert Verlag, Hamburg, and the Bertelsmann Lese-
ring. The English version was prepared by the author.

PREFACE

In the summer of 1957, my wife and I journeyed extensively through the German territories east of the Oder-Neisse line, which since the end of the second world war have been under Polish administration. Later during the same year my report of this journey, which had taken us from East Prussia via Danzig and Pomerania to East Brandenburg and Silesia, was published in West Germany in the form of a book entitled "Unter Polnischer Verwaltung", literally: Under Polish Administration.

Almost three years have passed since then. A little more information about this area has become available. It indicates that the substance of what was reported in 1957 remains the same.

On the 17th of October 1959, Mr. Wladyslaw Gomulka, the First Secretary of the United Polish Workers' Party (the Communist Party) addressed the party's Central Committee on the subject of the economic crisis facing Poland, the signs of which had become increasingly evident during the previous months. In this speech Mr. Gomulka made some telling points regarding the problems facing the Polish economy. Since 1956, Poland's supply of foodstuffs had been chiefly financed by means of foreign credits, he declared, and the country's balance of foreign trade showed this fact in the form of a considerable debit. As a result, the general standard of living would go down, Mr. Gomulka went on to predict. This prediction must apply particularly to the German territories under Polish administration. These large areas, laid waste by war, made desolate by years of partly deliberate and partly inevitable neglect, and devoid of their original population, have been a drag on Poland's economy; the country's investment potential is insufficient to provide needed capital, its industrial output incapable of supplying adequate machinery and goods, and the feeling of insecurity and strangeness of the area's new population had added to the problem.

As was to be expected, a detailed and documented account of conditions in the Polish administrated territories was not welcomed in communist Poland and my book aroused the wrath of the authorities. Frequent attempts were made to prove that I had made errors and deliberately distorted facts. Recently other reporters have been similarly accused: late in 1959 a correspondent of "The New York Times" well known for his conscientious and well-founded dispatches from Warsaw, was required to leave the country without a single news item for which he had been responsible being proven inaccurate. Reports by this correspondent and by other western newsmen indicate that the facts I gathered in 1957 have not lost their validity today. In two articles published in "The Guardian" in November 1959, a writer who had just visited the territories under Polish administration confirmed many of my impressions, adding: "The whole Silesian and Pomeranian regions show alarming signs of deterioration (in this respect the report written by Charles Wassermann, 'Unter Polnischer Verwaltung', is by no means exaggerated)."

In short, conditions have altered very little and in some instances they have worsened. Here and there some changes have taken place but unfortunately the total picture has remained the same. Hence, the present report stands as a reflection of conditions in this area today. Nor has the problem of the Oder-Neisse region lost its timeliness. Not only the Germans who have been driven from this land are concerned with its condition and the manner in which Poland administers this third part of the divided Germany. Beyond this question looms an even larger one: The German Peace Treaty and the final settlement of Germany's eastern boundary; for it is not only the future of Berlin and the Soviet Zone of Germany which remains to be settled, but also the fate of the German East.

This English version of my report will, I hope, serve as an aid for those who wish to concern themselves with the solution of one of the chief problems on which peace in Europe may hinge.

EAST PRUSSIA

"If something were to happen here, we Germans would again be the losers", said the East Prussian peasant. We had stopped at the outskirts of the town of Lyck, near the border between the Soviet Union and the German territories under Polish administration. He was one of the few Germans left in this area, one of the handful who had been able to stay on his land, despite difficulties and dangers. He looked at me, the reporter from the West, at Jacqueline, my wife, who sat next to me in our American car with its Canadian licence plate. "Today it isn't so much a question of the Poles persecuting us Germans", he said, "but the danger of the Russians coming back. And that can happen quite easily. In fact it's far more likely than you in the West think."

"Then what about the future?" I asked.

"Future? We don't have a real future, not now. We have nothing at all. And later,—oh well, we'll see. In any case I think it's best to get out of here while the going is good, before everything blows up in your face. That's what I say. There is no future here. Not right now anyway, perhaps never again."

He was tall and thin, with flashing blue eyes and the lined, leathery face of a man who works the land. He stood beside the car, leaning on his bicycle and it was clear that he was delighted to speak German, not only because we had come from the West like visitors from an other world, but also because speaking his native tongue was still something special; until a year ago it had hardly been possible and even now, as he put it, "you still have to be careful." As he spoke he kept looking around with watchful, steady eyes, and every time somebody came along the road and stopped to stare at the car, our conversation ended abruptly. "Someone from my village," he would whisper and we could be certain that the passer-by would be a Pole. In this area the Germans had to be sought out like needles in a haystack.

We had already driven several hundred miles through the German territories under Polish administration before meeting this man. The journey had begun in Warsaw.

We had left the hotel "Bristol", in which most foreign visitors were being lodged at the time, on a Saturday afternoon. As usual, the hotel had been full and, to the discomfiture of the guests, surrounded by a large scaffolding on which an army of workers clambered, scraped and hammered with abandon.

"We are building everywhere," an official of "Orbis", the state travel organization which manages the "Bristol" and other large hotels, had told me with some pride. "Poland will soon become a major tourist attraction."

We had wondered then, whether this new-found interest in reconstruction and the clearing away of the rubble of war would also be noticeable in other parts of the country. Two hours after leaving Warsaw we found the first answers to this question and began to make entries in our diaries.

"HERE LIES GERMAN,—FINISHED!"

Neidenburg.—This first village north of the former Polish-East-Prussian frontier is now named Nidzica. There, where the border once crossed the highway, a shield has been put up, marking the juncture of the "wojewodztwo" or province of Warsaw and the province of Olsztyn. The latter is named after its capital, the erstwhile German town of Allenstein. A short distance south of the border we saw a partially destroyed tower, which probably belonged to Poland's pre-1939 northern defence system. The further we drove away from Warsaw, the less road-traffic there was. In the border area there were no more passenger cars,—just a few old lorries. It is the same in Neidenburg. Here we have seen only two trucks; all other traffic consists of ancient, horse-drawn carts.

The center of Neidenburg is in ruins. The city hall is still more or less intact and apparently used to house government offices, but the roof and the upper storey have been severely damaged; most windows are broken and covered with newspaper. At the northern end of the town, near a level-crossing, there is a huge dump of scrap iron; the buildings around it,—all of them dirty and neglected,—look as though they once belonged to a large factory or warehouse. Few people are to be seen,—here and there small groups of young men in tattered clothing, who stand at street-corners, smoking and talking. As we pass, they turn to stare at us with unbelieving eyes.

Outside Neidenburg most buildings have been destroyed. The majority must have belonged to farms. Often only a heap of rubble, surrounded on all sides by neglected lilac bushes, gives evidence that a house once stood here. The living-quarters of these farms have suffered particularly, but nearby stables and barns did not fare much better: some are a total loss and the walls of others are in varying stages of decay.

Now we are about to leave the main highway to see a little more of the surrounding countryside.

North of Gilgenburg.—The little side road to Gilgenburg, which is now called Dabrowno, is very rough; we drove through pot holes which certainly had not been filled in for several years. In the village itself the cobble-stones are either very uneven, or missing altogether. The sign-posts along this road are hard to find; we had to stop frequently to ask for directions. Although we were well into former German territory, we could not find a single German. The Poles with whom we spoke could not speak German either; in central Poland many of them speak the language. The people here have broad, somewhat flat faces and we thought some looked Asiatic. They live in badly kept houses, some of which are near collapse. Since we could not get by with German, we tried our luck with our limited Polish: "Prosze bardzo, Dabrowno?" the reply was always very friendly, very long, and,—we were sure,—closely connected with the life-stories of our informants. Fortunately, we were also able to detect some recognizable gestures and a few words such as: "prosto", "na lewo" and "na prawo", which we were able to interpret as "straight ahead", "left" and "right" and can now include in our vocabulary.

Along the side road we saw fewer ruins, but *Gilgenburg* itself was in poor condition. On the market-square all the houses except a few on one side had disappeared. Even these were severely damaged.

There seems to be no thought of reconstruction in this area. Many of the ruins are overgrown with grass, and even the clearing of the rubble has not progressed beyond piling stones and bricks into heaps.

Now, past Gilgenburg our "mobile kitchen", has been put into service for the first time on this trip. We are having afternoon-coffee. We always carry "the kitchen" with us when in eastern Europe; it consists of two large suitcases, filled with imperishable foods, above all canned goods, with thermos bottles for coffee and soup and an electric heating device which can be connected to any power-source and provides us with hot water for beverages, washing and shaving. At over-night stops away from the big centers existing facilities rarely include such luxuries as hot water. Previous visits to Poland have taught us that there are few restaurants or hotels throughout the country where one can enjoy a meal.

The "Orbis" hotels are usually the best and we have already decided to use these as our headquarters wherever possible, even if this involves extra-trips to return to our accomodations. But there is no "Orbis" hotel in East Prussia and we will have to be satisfied with a hotel „Warminski" in Allenstein. According to information provided by Polish acquaintances in Warsaw the "Warminski" is supposed to be good, although we could find no one who had actually spent a night there. We shall see.

In the meantime we are in our "mobile coffee-house". Jacqueline has an extraordinary gift for making the most unusual places comfortable: the "coffee-house" (occasionally it also serves as "restaurant" and "breakfast room") has been set up in the front seat of the car. Between us a clean table-cloth has been spread; on it are plastic coffee-cups and plastic plates with sandwiches and biscuits. There are even some flowers to decorate our table.

Besides keeping our diaries up to date we are studying two road-maps, an old German one and a new Polish edition, trying to find a way to the Tannenberg memorial which is supposed to be somewhere in this area. The memorial, once famous throughout Germany, was built to commemorate fieldmarshal von Hindenburg's 1914 victory over tzarist Russia. We have never been in this region, neither before nor since the war, but have seen pictures of the memorial, a huge monument surrounded by elaborate parks. It would be interesting to know what it looks like today. Unfortunately the place is not shown on either of our maps; in fact the Polish map is only good for main-roads and indicates no villages nor roads in the area where we are now located. But still, we want to try and find our way. Perhaps an often repeated "Prosze bardzo" will help us again.

Hohenstein.—We discovered a village called Tannenberg on our German map, went there and learned that it was not the site of the memorial. We found a small hamlet, consisting of a handful of tumble-down houses. The Poles whom we had asked the way, evidently knew the word "Tannenberg" and had gladly directed us to the village. But when we had inquired where we might find the memorial by the same name, our conversations had inevitably broken down.

At last I remembered that in one of our innumerable suitcases there was an ancient Baedecker of Germany; it was in "the office", which contains books, papers, films and tapes, in fact everything a correspondent might possibly need in a region where there is nothing to buy.

Sure enough, there we found an explanation of how to get from the village of Tannenberg to the Tannenberg memorial. Simple: just go to Hohenstein. But where was Hohenstein? After scrutinizing our two maps, we discovered that the former Hohenstein is now called Olsztynek and that we were not far from it. To be on the safe side we drove back to the main road Warsaw-Danzig and then followed our Polish map. Soon we reached Hohenstein.

After the very short time we have spent in East-Prussia up to now, we nonetheless feel that we have seen the first indication of what might be a general rule: in small towns and villages the center of the community is usually in ruins and there is little or no evidence of reconstruction. Yet some of the most important public buildings,—the churches and the city hall,—often still exist, even if they have suffered considerable damage.

In Hohenstein the same applied. The church steeple could be seen a long way off, because the buildings which once surrounded it have completely disappeared. The church even seemed to be in good condition. After cruising around for some minutes we stopped at one rubble-filled street corner; nearby we saw another of the ubiquitous groups of idle young men. Again they stopped their conversation as we approached and stared incredulously. I drove a little closer to them and asked in German if they could direct me to the Tannenberg memorial.

One of the young men came to the window and spoke to me in halting but intelligible German. There was a strong smell of vodka on his breath and I wondered if he would have been as ready to speak German had he not drunk what was obviously a sizeable amount of Poland's national beverage. He was friendly and suggested that he could easily show us the way if I would let him come with us in the car.

While the smell of vodka dit not frighten us, it nonetheless caused a defence mechanism to be put into action: we mumbled something about the lack of space for an extra passenger,—an exaggeration although it had some basis in fact,—and asked the man to be good enough to give us a verbal explanation. He was visibly disappointed but complied.

Today the Tannenberg memorial is nothing but a heap of rubble and wasteland. The monument itself looks like a vulcanic crater, the surrounding parks have turned into wild thickets with occasional patches of sparse grass. On one side there is a wheat field. According to the old photograph which we had with us, a broad drive-way once led to the center of the memorial. It has become a small path, criss-crossed by the tracks of waggon wheels, which leads to the edge of the crater. As I looked at these vast ruins I suddenly remembered how they had been created: this was one of those last acts of Adolf Hitler at the end of his dreadful reign. When he knew the war was lost and German troups had to retreat towards the West, he sent a special detachment of men to Hohenstein with the sole task of blowing up the Tannenberg memorial. The job was thoroughly done. The brickwork has all but gone. Only in the center of the crater is there one recognizeable reminder of what all this once looked like: lying face down, surrounded by rubble, there is a huge statue of field-marshall Hindenburg. Two of these once guarded the center-piece of the memorial. One has vanished, the other could hardly lie in a more symbolic position.

In the former park we met two people: where we left the car, an old Polish peasant in leather-boots, a thick jacket buttoned up to his chin and a tattered blue cap on his head, watched over a cow and two horses which alternatively grazed and, like their guardian, stared at us. Nearer the monument an equally old man stood motionless while a lean white goat, which he held on a leash, grazed among meagre tufts of grass. He was very pleased to have his photograph taken and delighted when I offered him a cigarette. At first it appeared that he did not understand a word of German and when I tried with the help of gestures to find out if he knew what the destroyed monument had once represented, he replied merely with a toothless grin. Then he pointed at the fallen statue and managed a few words of German after all:

"Here lies German,—finished!" and again he smiled cheerfully.

His words had not been spoken in an unfriendly tone but rather as if he had wanted to give me an important piece of information.

When we returned to our car, about ten children were playing around it. They stepped aside politely as we approached. Jacqueline asked the old peasant who was still standing nearby, if there was a way of getting some drinking water, for whenever possible we want to save our supply of coffee and fruit juice for emergencies. The peasant seemed to understand her sign-language and despatched one of the children who soon returned with a pot of water. The water was so dirty, that in order not to insult the peasant we went to the other side of the car and pretended to drink while really rinsing our hands. In this region particular care will evidently be necessary regarding drinking water; even in Warsaw most people avoid it, preferring soda- and mineral water. Here, among the ruins of war and neglect, the situation will surely be much worse.

Now, as we have completed our notes and are ready to leave the Tannenberg memorial and Hohenstein, the cow and the two horses are thoughtfully climbing the moss-covered steps from the road to the former park. Clearly they plan to keep the white goat company.

We are off, towards Allenstein.

Allenstein.—We reached the hotel "Warminski" around 10 o'clock last night. From the outside the building looks fairly new. It is a four-storey structure which seems unfinished because it lacks a coat of mortar over its bare brick walls. Many houses in Warsaw and other Polish cities have the same appearance. But the inside of the "Warminski" is quite finished,—though not in the usual sense of the word: the walls and ceilings are already crumbling.

But I did not see the inside right away, because first we went into our standard routine for arrivals at East-European hotels: Jacqueline went inside to make sure that the rooms we had reserved were really available and to ascertain if the place was at all inhabitable (we had learned to expect some considerable surprises in this connection). In the meantime I guarded the car, which was soon surrounded by a large crowd, even at this time of the night. I also busied myself preparing our gear for removal to the hotel: the cameras and tape-recorder, which could never be left in the car over night, and a selection of suitcases called the "short stay group", including that part of "the kitchen" needed to prepare our soup and coffee for the next day. The rest of our luggage,—and there is always a lot more,— is then kept in the car's large and securely locked trunk from where it can be fetched as needed.

A few minutes later Jacqueline returned and reported:

"We have a room. It's very small and shabby but comparatively clean. We can even get something to eat, but in a room in which an orchestra plays dance-music until two in the morning. Nobody in the hotel can think of a place where there might be a garage, but perhaps it will be possible to find something later on. The hotel desk is on the first floor, and the two women there speak no German, English, or French. But they fetched a guest, who speaks a little German and he has been a helpful interpreter.

Now we began the second phase of our arrival-routine: Jacqueline stayed with the car and I carried the luggage to the hotel reception.

I was shown to our room. Indeed it was no bigger than a small prison-cell.

Downstairs the walls fairly shook with noise. The dining-room was here, complete with dance orchestra, and a large crowd which not only danced with violent abandon but, judging by the people who came outside for a breath of fresh air, also drank with equal enthusiasm. At the foot of the stairs, near the swinging doors to the dining room, a dozen or more men swayed and staggered around. Others left the hotel and formed an unsteady circle around our car. I decided to do everything possible to find a garage.

As I came to the car to fetch a third load of baggage, someone spoke to me in flawless German:

"You will certainly want to put that car away, won't you?" I looked

15

around and saw a young man, perhaps in his mid-twenties, who stood beside me and smiled.

"Yes," I replied, "if I had a garage."

"You certainly can't leave the car here," he went on, "or they'll steal everything from it that they can move. Try and find a garage through the hotel. And in the meantime park the car around the corner, over there, in that empty lot. I'll stay with it and take care that no one does any harm."

"Thank's, but why should you do a thing like that?" I protested.

"Oh, it's really a pleasure," he said, then came very close to me and whispered:

"I am an old Allensteiner."

I drew back in surprise: his breath reeked of vodka and now I also noticed that he swayed visibly as he leaned towards me. This increased my determination to find a garage. Returning to the hotel, I asked for the guest who had been Jacqueline's interpreter. He turned out to be cooperative and promised to help. He disappeared into the office behind the reception desk and returned to report that a place had been found in the "party-garage", not a hundred yards from the hotel. Soon our car stood peacefully next to the vehicles of the communist party of Poland.

Then the interpreter-guest lead us to the restaurant.

The room was filled to overflowing, the atmosphere hot and stifling. The orchestra played with a violence as if the musician's lives depended on it and several hundred dancers, showing equally grim determination, screamed and leaped around a tiny dance floor.

Our interpreter brought us a young waitress who, he said, would be able to understand and look after us. Wishing us a good night's rest, he bowed and left. We felt there was good reason for the fame of Polish hospitality.

The waitress, a girl of about twenty, spoke very good German. After considerable trouble she managed to find a table for us. The food she brought was simple but tasty. With it we drank a watery yet palatable beer.

The girl had to serve many tables, but every time she came to us we exchanged a few sentences. It was clear that Polish was the language which she spoke more fluently; she had an indefinable accent in German and frequently made grammatical errors, but had no trouble expressing herself. When I commented on her fluency in German, she looked at me with evident surprise.

"But I am German," she said.

"You mean, Masurian?" I asked, thinking of a group of people in southern East Prussia. The Masurians were of both Polish, and German ancestry, but many were germanized in the early twentieth century.

"Yes, but German," she replied emphatically. Then she had to rush away once more.

Later that evening I had several other occasions to talk to her. Her parents, she told me, still lived in Allenstein; she herself was born and brought up here. Between 1945, when she was still very young, and 1956, German had hardly been spoken in her home, because it had been too dangerous. Now it could be risked again, but in the intervening years she had forgotten a lot. Her parents scolded her these days, she said, pointing out that she should make an effort to perfect her German again, but until now she had had very few opportunities. There was too much work, she said, and too few people who dared to speak German in public.

"In other cities it's supposed to be much easier," she told me, "but Allenstein is the capital of a wojewodztwo, and here the Poles have been after us Germans for so long, most of us have lost all enthusiasm for speaking our language."

This conversation reminded me of those national groups to which the Poles have given the collective name "outochthones" (derived from the Greek word meaning original inhabitants). To these belong the people from Masuria and Ermland in East Prussia, the Kaschubes from the region which, between the two world wars, was called the Polish corridor, the "Slowinzen", a small minority which lived around

17

the Pommeranian town of Köslin, and the inhabitants of eastern Upper Silesia. These racial groups have been an ethnic, sociological and frequently also a political problem for some decades. They are minorities which sometimes have been called Slavs and therefore Poles; on other occasions they declared themselves voluntarily as Poles, for the understandable reason that they hoped thereby to make their political future more secure; then again they were called Germans, or preferred to be called so. During the first years of Polish administration of the former German areas, the Polish authorities decided to recognize the autochtones as Slavs, chiefly because it was thought that such a move would strenghten Poland's legal claim to these regions. It is known that by no means all autochthones where willing to accept this policy. In the years of violent persecution of Germans, many autochthones, particularly the Masurians, courageously identified themselves with their German forbearers. Then a decision was taken in Warsaw: the autochthones, it was declared, could not really be called proper Slavs and should therefore receive no more consideration than the Germans.

Thus the fortunes of the autochthones altered from year to year, determined in part by their own decisions, in part by the policies of the governments under which they had to live.

These general facts where known to us before we came to East Prussia. But the declaration by the young waitress, that she was Masurian and German, appeared to me as the first material proof of a claim often heard in Germany today: that many autochthones considered themselves a suppressed minority in present-day Poland. Perhaps we will find more evidence to support this claim.

At the beginning of the year 1957 the cost-of-living for foreigners visiting Poland became more reasonable. Earlier the official exchange rate for the Zloty had been pegged to the russian Rouble and one Dollar bought four Zloty (while banks in some neutral western countries were glad to be rid of their Zloty holdings at 130 to the

Dollar). Now the official rate is 24 Zloty. While this improvement in favor of foreigners is most useful for us, the cost of living for Poles continues to be very high.

We were made aware of this on the evening of our arrival, during a conversation we had with the manager—he is actually called the director—of the hotel dining-room. He was a blond young man, in his early thirties, who came to our table and greeted us courteously. We invited him to sit with us and he accepted but would not have a drink.

"When I have duty, I drink not," he explained in halting but intelligible German. We soon learned that he could speak the language because he had been in Austria as a prisoner-of-war. In due course a discussion about a variety of subjects ensued, while the restaurant pulsated to the "hot licks" of jazz-in-the-Allenstein-manner and the shrieks and thumps of the dancing multitude.

The manager did not hesitate to tell us about his life, and we were soon talking about prices and the standard of living. The man works from seven in the morning until eight in the evening with night duty until well after midnight every second evening. His pay of 2,000 Zloty a month is insufficient to support him, his wife and their three children. Therefore his wife, who—as he told us proudly—is a high school graduate, has taken a job in an office, for which she is paid 1,000 Zloty a month. In this way the family manages to get by. But there was cause for concern: with both parents going to work, two of their children spent the hours between the end of school, early in the afternoon, and the mother's return from her work, playing in the streets without any supervision. Only the third was young enough to be kept in a kindergarden all day.

"We know not what we should do," the manager said, "should we not have enough money, or should we leave the children alone for so many hours?

The dance roared on around us. Occasionally our companion was called away but always returned to our table. And so our conversation continued until two in the morning.

Like most new inhabitants of Allenstein the manager came from eastern Poland. He had been forced to leave the town of Wilna when it, along with a large portion of eastern Poland, had been taken over by the Russians. He had been in Allenstein for eleven years and had grown to like the town and its surroundings. One could not say the same thing about all new citizens in the area, he said; many were unhappy and longed for their original home. This was the reason, he thought, for the difficulties which had been encountered in agriculture in what was now called "the newly re-won territories"—,the former German provinces which the Poles now claim as permanently theirs. The new settlers, we were told, had usually not been given much land of their own, but had been made members of collective farms or they had become workers in "P.G.R." enterprises,—state-owned and operated farms. Many of these people had had no interest in agriculture, large numbers of them having come from big eastern cities, and even if they were farmers they had felt like strangers on the new land. There had also been a lack of incentive to work hard. Only the Masurians, many of whom had also been forced to become farm workers, had been more successful, the manager thought, for they had always been here and had felt closer to this country, to its earth.

But now it was hoped that agriculture would improve in this region. Peasants from southern Poland, from the region around Cracow were being settled in the north, and it was said that these people were more interested in agriculture and would surely improve production. Furthermore, an agricultural school had lately been established in a former insane asylum in Allenstein, and it too would help to improve the situation.

We were also told that Allenstein presently had a larger population than before the war. This was due to its role as a provincial capital, which had caused an influx of burocrats and their families. There were hardly any industries in and around the city, the manager told us, and until the end of 1956 there had been no private enterprises. But since the October-revolution in 1956, and the appointment of

Wladyslaw Gomulka as First Secretary of the communist party of Poland, many changes had taken place. Taxis had been the first private enterprises in Allenstein. Today there were already seventy of them. Several private shops had also been established but were finding it difficult to remain in business; it was practically impossible for them to compete with state-shops from which they had to purchase every article for resale.

As midnight passed and more and more guests swayed drunkenly around the room, we came to talk about alcoholism. The manager told us that vodka constituted the gravest social problem in Allenstein. Boys and girls still in their 'teens were turning into drunkards, and a great effort would somehow have to be made to stop this. The first counter-measure was an edict forbidding the sale of vodka in public places on Saturday night.

I asked how it could then be possible that on this evening, a Saturday, so many people were drunk. The manager shrugged his shoulders. "They bring it in," he said in a resigned tone, "this I cannot stop." It was clear that he was most concerned about the condition of so many of his guests. "I hope the next years will bring improvement," he added.

He was a member of the communist party, he told us, going on to express his conviction that, since Gomulka was the leader, the party and with it the whole nation was in good hands. When I asked the reason for this opinion he replied:

"Some things one knows, one feels them."

At two o'clock in the morning Jacqueline and I decided we were now tired enough to be able to sleep in the baby bath tub-like contraptions, which were supposed to be our beds. The manager accompanied us to the first floor and told us he would come to the hotel the next morning to show us around Allenstein. Having previously learned that he was ordinarily not on duty on Sunday mornings we had protested against this offer, but he would not change his mind. He wanted to be certain, he declared, that we saw the town properly, and also to supervise the preparation of the food supplies which we had ordered for our mid-day meal (we had decided to drive on after seeing Allenstein).

"I must be looking after you!" he said and beamed at us. Then, as a final thought he ordered a bucket of water to be sent to our room, for in Allenstein the water supply is turned off at 11 p.m.

One can even sleep quite well in baby bath tubs, provided one stays up long enough the evening before. This morning we awoke at seven o'clock, feeling remarkably refreshed. We are sure that part of the reason for our sound sleep is the fact that we have brought along our own bed linen with which we could cover the grey-white, torn sheets and pillow cases provided by the hotel.

Upon waking up we always follow another fixed routine: the "kitchen" is opened and our electric heater put to service to boil a large quantity of water. Our thermos bottles are then filled with soup and coffee. While Jacqueline attends to this, it is my job to shine our shoes and brush our clothes; we pay particular attention to these details, knowing that this is a way of staving off depression which, once it has set in, is most difficult to eradicate.

In the hotel restaurant we ordered bread, butter, boiled eggs and hot water. Even in the restaurants we prepare our own instant coffee. It is both better and cheaper.

Meanwhile the dining room manager had arrived with his little son. He ordered our supplies including twelve small bottles of soda water, which I had asked for after our experience of the previous day. When I inquired about other hotels in East Prussia where we might stay, the manager spoke glowingly of a "wonderful place" in Gizycko (the former Lötzen), in which we would certainly find good accomodation. We decided to pay our bill in Allenstein and take all our things along, but, in order to be on the safe side, told the desk clerk that we might return that evening. Fortunately a woman was now on duty who seemed to understand our plans.

Allenstein looked less neglected than the other east Prussian towns we had seen to date. A large number of houses was missing in the center, but the ruins had been cleared away, and, the manager told us, it is planned to rebuild the old city exactly as it was before the war. The best known public buildings, the churches, the "New City Hall" and the castle are undamaged or already rebuilt.

We visited the castle and climbed the famous Copernicus tower (the Polish astronomer completed some of his studies here), and were rewarded with a fine view of the city. While Jacqueline returned to the car, the manager, his son and I wandered through the streets. We passed a protestant church near the castle. I entered and found Sunday morning service in progress. The pastor delivered his sermon in Polish. Near one of the catholic churches I found a shop with a sign "Ars christiana" over its entrance, where religious articles were sold.

"A year ago this shop was not here," said the manager.

I took some photographs and then we returned to the car. The manager led us to the eastern exit from Allenstein. We left the town at 11:30 a.m., and are now heading east, towards Sensburg and Lyck. En route Jacqueline made the following notes in her diary:

Shortly after returning to the car in Allenstein I was addressed in French:

"You're from Canada, perhaps you speak French?"

A young man in worn-out blue overalls stood beside me. I told him that I do indeed, since I am French-Canadian. He was delighted.

"Oh, to have a chance to speak French again!" he exclaimed. He had no accent whatever. Then in short sentences, breathlessly, as if he wanted to unburden himself as quickly as possible, he told me the following:

"My family comes from south-east Poland. I was a small child when we emigrated to France. My father worked in the coal mines. I was brought up as a Frenchman. My sister was born in France. After the end of the second world war my father suddenly discovered that he was homesick, and we returned to Poland. But the native land my father sought did not exist any more; it had become Soviet Russia. So we were sent to this part of the country. We don't like it here.

This is no more my father's native land than France was. And me,
I long to be back in France. We don't live well here, life is hard,—
very hard.
"One day my sister said she couldn't stand it any more. So she asked
for a passport to go back to France. Just about then she fell in love
with a young chap here,—and a short while later her application
for a passport was granted. Because she couldn't stand living here
any more, and in the hope that her fiancé would be able to follow
her, she decided to leave. But this chap is a skilled worker; he'll
never get a passport. My sister is back in France now. She is doing
quite well,—she has a motor scooter; but her heart is broken."
He sighed and added: "I wish I was in her place. Many of us would
like to be in her shoes. La vie est dure, madame, dure."
Then, as if he was much relieved because he had told me his story,
the young man shook my hand fervently and hurried away.

We have just stopped for lunch. The next larger town will be Sensburg. From there we plan to drive through the lake district to Lyck, not far from the Russian border.

"NOW HE'S OFF TO GERMANY!"

En route to Sensburg.—We are reminded of what the restaurant manager told us about the plight of agriculture in this district. The fields are in poor condition. Some were ploughed this spring or perhaps last autumn, but no crop was sowed. Grass and weeds are groving in the furrows.

Warthenburg,—now called Barczewo,—consists partly of ruins, partly of houses in neglected condition. Jacqueline has a look at the market square and says:
"Whoever lives here now doesn't love this little town."
She is right. The houses look unloved. The only bright spot in Wartenburg: a few children in Polish folk costumes. Perhaps the authorities want to encourage a new folk tradition.

Bischofsburg (Biskupiec) is also full of ruins, but the market square is being newly paved and a few houses are under repair. There are many soldiers about.

Sensburg,—now renamed Mragowo,—is still said to be what it was in German times: an important settlement of protestant Masurians. As we drive through this town on one of the countless east prussian lakes, our tape recorder is turned on and takes down our immediate impressions:

Here, too, whole blocks of houses have been destroyed. Bricks and other building materials have been collected into heaps but not removed. Especially the larger houses, which once must have been surrounded by attractive gardens, have either been destroyed completely or are severely damaged. The gardens have become a wilderness. No traffic at all here. Quite a few pedestrians, who stop and stare as we pass. Up to now we haven't heard a word of German. Nothing more to see here. We'd better continue east. But unfortunately I forgot to buy gasoline in Allenstein. The tank is nearly empty. I have an emergency supply of two five-gallon cans in the trunk, but don't want to use them if it can be avoided. Perhaps I can find a station here.—There, ahead, there's a primitive-looking pump! But it's Sunday! The state-owned gasoline stations—of course there are no private ones,—are closed on Sundays; especially outside the larger cities. Oh well, let's continue! The trouble is, we won't get far this way. Polish gasoline has a very low octane content,—I've noticed, we need almost a third more per mile than when we use western fuel. But over there, there is a pump in operation after all! A bus is filling up just now.

But,—no luck. This pump is only for state-owned vehicles. Too bad! Lot of young men around our car just now. Some of them are near the window. They speak German.

"I suppose you want gasoline?"—That was one of the young men. Interesting: he speaks fluently without a trace of an accent,—yet some of the words sound as if a Pole had spoken them.

"Yes, I'd like to tank up,—if I could buy some."

Now there are seven or eight young men at my window. They don't speak Polish among themselves. They discuss whether it might be possible to find the man in charge of the gas pump for private cars. At last they decide it ought to be possible.

"If you take us along, we'll see that you get gasoline."

"Alright, but I can't take all of you,—the most I have room for is one."

Laughter. "Oh well, we tried!"

Again a discussion: who will drive with us? The choice is soon made. A tall chap with a crew-cut. He sits next to Jacqueline.

"Lucky fellow! Now he's off to Germany!" One of those remaining behind calls out.—Tape off.

We've just driven back part of the way through Sensburg.

Now we've stopped at a street corner and our guide has run off to the house of the man in charge of the pump for private cars.

While we drove, I turned the tape recorder off, in order not to inhibit the young man. Now I can catch up and record what was said: He told us about life in Sensburg: There are apparently more Germans here than Poles. When he says "Germans" he means Masurians. But quite a lot of them have emigrated from here recently, for during the last year it's again been possible to get travel papers to go to the west. Sensburg once had a population of 11,000. Now there are only 7,000 left, more than half of them Masurians.

The young man will also emigrate shortly. Together with his mother he will go to the "DDR", East Germany, where his father has lived since the end of the war. He is glad to be able to get away from here. "Life is hopeless here," he said. "I earn 400 to 500 Zloty a month as a house painter's apprentice, and this jacket I have on costs 350 Zloty. A pound of bacon costs 20 Zloty. I earn a little extra money by accepting private jobs a a painter after my regular work. But still I don't earn enough to live."

I asked if he didn't think that there might be an improvement soon. "Improvement isn't the right word," he replied. "During the past year and a half the Poles have cancelled a number of the anti-German laws. But until there's a noticeable improvement, another hundred years will have to pass!"

My next question referred to the relations between Masurians and Poles.

"We don't have much to do with one another," shrugged the young Masurian, "except that we play soccer with them since a little while. Before that there were two soccer teams here, both mixed. But the Poles play less and less and now they only have one team which is all Polish; meanwhile we've put together our own team. Recently we began calling our team "Mazur" and they didn't stop us.— We beat them every Sunday," he added, "but most of us don't enjoy that particularly. We'd all rather be outside."

I asked what he meant by "outside": the "DDR" or the Federal Republic of Germany.

"Oh well, any old place in the Reich," he replied.

Evidently the "Reich" continues to be a meaningful term in the thinking of these people, although it has long ceased to exist as a political entity.

When we had reached the street corner where we are still standing, a group of about eight girls passed by, heard that we were speaking German, stopped and joined in the conversation. In no time we had learnt that three of them were due to leave Sensburg with their families within two weeks to emigrate to the Federal Republic. "We are counting the hours," they said.

Nowadays, they told us, it only takes a few months before most applications for travel documents are granted. However, one had to have relatives in Germany.

"But in a way we've been waiting twelve years for our documents," said the oldest of the girls; she was perhaps twenty years old.

Again we noted that the girls spoke fluent German, but nonetheless made the odd grammatical error or mispronounced a word. I asked how it was that they still spoke German at all; they told me that they all spoke it at home. Just the same, it had been difficult not to forget the language during all the past years. There had been no German schools in Sensburg, nor was there one now, and until a year ago it had been practically impossible to speak German in public.

"We've mixed up our language a lot," the oldest girl said. "Writing in German is something we've completely forgotten. Our friends, who've already emigrated to Germany still write us letters in Polish. But in time they'll learn to write German again, and we too,—once were outside."

The girls told us that most Masurians had never agreed to the polonization programme enforced by the authorities,—even when the pressure had been greatest. They recalled a time when groups of people had gathered in front of the militia headquarters and sung German songs. "And nothing happened to them,—because the militia couldn't lock up everybody!" they said.

Beyond this they were reluctant to speak of the past. Only the future really interested them. They too said that they did not care where they would end up, as long as it was "outside", and were ready to accept a stay in one of West Germany's rufugee clearing camps as part of the process of emigration. Then they asked us about life in the West; there where countless things they wanted to know; one question had been put to us frequently in all the iron curtain countries: "how much does your car cost in the West?" A private automobile has become the symbol of western wealth throughout eastern Europe; it causes more attention and is more eagerly inspected and discussed than anything else a western visitor might bring along.

The young people of Sensburg asked their questions in a far less resigned tone than was usually the case, for over and over again the words: "oh well, soon we'll find out for ourselves" and "soon we'll be under way too" were interspersed among the inquires.

Before the girls left us, some of them suggested it might be best if they simply climbed into our trunk to go "outside' as soon as possible. I've just had enough time to record all this. Here comes our young man, together with another,—obviously the man for the pump.— End of the tape recording.

On the way to Lyck.—We managed to get a tank-full of gasoline, then said good-bye to our Masurian friend, giving him the present which is by far the best for anyone in these parts: cigarettes.

Along the highway we again saw a large number of lilacs which enclosed squares consisting only of heaps of rubble. We also passed a collective farm. A herd of black-and-white cattle and some horses grazed around new but unpainted farm buildings. The cattle was dirty but well fed. The horses were in excellent health. The grazing grounds were spare, with sandy patches appearing at frequent intervals. Near these meadows we once more saw ploughed land were no crops had been sowed.

Collective and state farms have become an increasing liability to Poland, a fact freely admitted by the authorities in Warsaw. Moreover, it would be quite right to say, that every form of agricultural production faces crises.

In all parts of the country the peasants have taken advantage of the opportunity given them by the Gomulka administration: they have resigned from the collectives in droves and returned to private farming. The collectives were in difficulties long before the Gomulka era, and now, with fewer members and less land, their condition is worse than ever. But private farm production has by no means improved correspondingly. In part this is due to crop-hoarding by farmers, who count on being able to force an increase in prices. The government has tried to resist this pressure. At present, in the summer of 1957, it cannot be said that the government has implemented all the changes the people—particularly the peasants—had excepted. Still, Gomulka has given private farmers their first glimmer of hope for a better life since the advent of communism in Poland; hence they continue to have faith in him. Ironically enough, the farmers' feeling of greater freedom after years of forced membership in collectives or bitter fights against rigid delivery quotas, has led to the "hamster" practices and a price war, particularly in grains.

The situation is worsened by the general protest of the great majority of peasants,—whether they are private or in collectives,—against the entire body of communist agricultural policy; this protest takes the form of planting as little as can be planted, doing, in fact the least possible amount of work without incurring the wrath of the all-powerful state. The final blow is the great difficulty encountered in the former german territories, where new settlers are expected to produce agricultural products in a land to which they have neither purely practical nor emotional ties. Hardly any aspect of agriculture in Poland has been spared by this general crisis; certainly it is not limited to the so-called "socialist sector". Moreover, the crisis had developped to such an extent, that today Poland is forced to import grain, although it once was an important exporter of the same product, and a reporter travelling through this country soon notices frequent manifestations of this situation: fallow land where there should be vast grain fields.

In the small village of *Barranoven*—its polish name is Baranowo—the attractive old church has escaped all but minor damage, yet nearby a large estate has been completely destroyed.
Shortly after Barranoven we drove through a very small village. On one building we noticed in large, though by now barely legible letters the word "Raiffeisen". This was the first German sign (it refers to the Raiffeisen cooperative savings banks throughout Germany) we had seen in the former german territories under Polish administration.

Arys—now called Orzysz—seems to have become a Polish garrison town. Although a large number of buildings has been destroyed, most houses along the main street are still more or less intact or have been replaced by wooden temporary structures. All shop windows are protected by sturdy irons bars, and soon one sees the reason for such a measure: the streets are filled with soldiers, many of them in advanced stages of drunkenness. As we stopped at a closed level crossing just outside Arys, we saw a drunken soldier who lay head downward in the deep ditch beside the road. Once again we were reminded of the restaurant manager in Allenstein and his worried remarks concerning alcoholism.

"THEY'LL NEVER CUT UP MY CAP AGAIN!"

Lyck.—Our current rest period was over-due. We have already driven a long way today and have seen and experienced a lot, especially right here in Lyck. This town near the eastern end of East Prussia has been renamed Elk.

On arrival, I took some general snapshots. Along the main street, which runs above the shore line of a picturesque lake, there are the usual gaps in the rows of houses, with their casually piled up heaps of rubble, bricks and stones. The former protestant parish church, a large structure on the main street, has evidently been renovated recently and is now used for roman catholic services. I also saw another undamaged church steeple at a distance. But by and large the town, particularly its western section, is most depressing. In one of the larger bombed out lots, a horse grazed where it could find a few tufts of grass. I studied my Baedecker and realized all this was once a built-up area; here stood houses, people lived and worked here and now only a horse fed there,—the unknowing symbol of destruction and decay. Wherever I took pictures I was surrounded by a group of dirty, barefoot children. Their physiognomies seemed east-European and their totally shorn heads contributed to this impression.

Between the former protestant church and the lake not a single house is still standing, although the Baedecker lists several blocks of business and residential buildings. In this vast sea of rubble, on the slope towards the lake, I found a sad spot: under some low bushes and some broken bricks were the remains of an old wall; it enclosed what must have been the formal garden of a villa. There was no trace of the house, but I came upon an almost perfectly preserved fountain in a marble basin and near it, a stone bench. I photographed this,—not so much out of sentimentality, but because I had found a visually powerful example of the immense and all-pervading changes which have taken place in this land in little more than a decade.

As I was looking for the best camera angle, I heard footsteps behind me and an excited voice called out in Polish. I turned to find a small,

31

positively hungry looking man in a tattered and dirty blue suit and a shirt without collar, who was hurrying towards me. His sallow face and blue-green eyes showed alarm; he urgently wanted to see or know something. His self-important manner, had the effect of annoying me before I really knew why. I went on taking photographs and gave the man to understand that I had no idea what he wanted. Thereupon he switched to a mixture of Polish and German and his purpose became clear: who I was, why was I in Lyck, or rather Elk, and why and with whose permission was I taking pictures? An inquisition of this kind inevitably causes the same reaction in me: I become rude, very supercilious and, above all, I treat the questioner like a two year old child.

"Alright, alright," I said, "my documents are in order, don't worry," and I went on with my work.

The man became even more excited and demanded to know further details.

"Look, will you leave me alone so I can get on with my work?" I said then. "If you're so keen to see my documents, then run over there to my car,—there you can read everything you want."

The man murmured a few words of protest, but I paid no further attention. Soon he turned and went back to the street. Later Jacqueline told me that he had looked her and the car over before coming to me, but had not returned. We did not see him again. We are not sure whether he was a policeman in civilian clothes, an informer or simply an over-anxious type. If he really was a policeman, which I consider quite likely, then one thing ought to be emphasized: the undiplomatic, in fact, unwise manner in which I dealt with him would have had much more serious consequences in any other eastern European country, —and also in Poland before the 1956 October Revolution; there can be no doubt that this has become considerably less of a police state. Ten minutes later we stopped in another part of Lyck. As so often before, our car served as an excellent means of attracting attention and brought us into contact with people. In this case chance would have it that we were surrounded by a number of people who spoke

German. At first the usual happened: the initial subject of conversation was the car and its price in the West. Then I said:
"I hear that soon there are to be more private cars in Poland."
"There's quite a few already," replied a man in colloquial German, "but a car like this one we won't get in a hundred years."
The man who had spoken stood on the fringe of the group around us. He was leaning on the saddle of his bicycle and smiled in a friendly way. He wore leather riding boots, heavy grey trousers and an old but still well preserved woolen coat which reached below his waist and was cut like a riding jacket. He was tall and thin, with flashing blue eyes and the lined, leathery face of a man who works the land. While the conversation continued he specialized in adding sarcastic comments. A Pole, speaking German with a strong accent, told us how the russian army had entered Lyck and set countless fires by means of hand granades and gasoline poured over the walls.
"They set fires where they felt like it, and as much as possible," the Pole said. Whereupon the German added:
"And now these ruins are being kept for ever and a day, so that we can have a nice memorial." He winked at me and turned the corners of his mouth downward in deprecation.
For a while we continued to chat avoiding controversial issues, as we always do here when talking to a larger group.
I had parked on the left side of the street. There is so little traffic, one tends to become careless about regulations. Suddenly a black "Warsawa"—the polish version of the russian "Pobieda" car—came down the street and passed us slowly by.
"That's a police car," the German with the bicycle said quietly. "You are parked on the left side, and that will give them a good reason to poke their noses into your documents."
Less out of fear than in the hope of being able to avoid a long session with the police, we bade the group around us farewell and drove on. The road signs indicating the route to Lötzen were sparse to say the least. We soon realized that somewhere we had taken a wrong turn. As I tried to decide how best to get back to the right road, a bicyclist

stopped beside me. It was the German whose whimsical comments I had noticed before.

"I did want to talk to you a little more," he said, "but when there are so many people around it's impossible to say anything. Particularly since they were Poles."

"You don't trust the Poles?" I asked.

"Oh well!" he replied and shrugged. An then he began to talk freely: He was a native of East Prussia, married, with three children. He had served in the German army during the second world war and was wounded. At the end of the war he had found himself in Mecklenburg, but because he did not like the Soviet Zone of Germany, had left and managed to get back to his native region. His decision to make this move had been strengthened by the fact that his brother, who had remained on the family farm while he had been away, was not interested in farming and wanted to do something else. And after all, someone had to remain on the land.

"I have forty three hectares," (about 107 acres) he said, "but I only work eight of them (about 20 acres) today. The rest I have leased out to a P.G.R., one of those state farms, although they hardly pay any rent. But I can't work more than eight hectares without hired hands. And I'm not allowed to hire anyone on, or else they'll call me a kulak right away.

"And believe me, it wasn't easy even to keep those eight hectares! To succeed, I had to run from pillar to post and give every second burocrat a . . . well, how would you call it . . . a present. Then, at long last, they let me stay on my own land,—which most other Germans weren't permitted to do. A little later, about three years ago, they came along and wanted to collect new taxes. They managed to figure out such an enormous amount that I would have had to sell all my moveables,—furniture and all,—to be able to pay them off. So I started to run form pillar to post again, and this time I went as far as Warsaw. And at the end they cancelled most of the new taxes again. That's the way things are here: every day something new, and always a mix-up, the likes of which you can't imagine. It's terrible!

34

"And in all this time, I'll tell you,—I got to know the inside of every prison in this district. It wasn't very pleasant, you may be sure of that."

He was standing very close to me and spoke calmly and quietly,— not secretively, but softly enough to make it hard for a passer-by to hear his words. Nonetheless in due couse there were quite a few people around us once more, and the usual questions about the car and its technical data began.

"I could tell you a lot more," he said, "but here it's impossible. You never know how people think. Not even nowadays."

Jacqueline and I were of two minds what to do. On the one hand we wanted to continue our conversation, on the other hand we did not want to cause trouble for the farmer, either by urging him to say more in the midst of a potential audience or by suggesting another rendez-vous and being overheard. Our problem was soon solved. He was now going to cycle to his house, which was located in a village near Lyck, the farmer said, adding very quietly, that if we wanted to follow him, we might stop for another chat. We gladly accepted and while he pedalled ahead, followed, trying to be unobtrusive, but aware that we were arousing the usual amount of attention.

On the outskirts of Lyck, the man dismounted and we were able to talk for some time without interruption.

He told us that his father now lived in a city in West Germany and that his wife and children had been there on a visit during the past spring. He, however, had not been granted a passport, in order to make sure that his family would return. Now, this summer, his brother would have an opportunity to visit their father, but would also return. Towards the end of the year he himself planned to go to the West and, if possible, make the necessary preparations for moving the entire family to the Federal Republic. The latest regulations issued by the polish authorities might make this possible.

"Since Gomulka there have been some improvements. But, you know, I've had enough!" he said. I asked what improvements there had been, and he told me:

"It isn't so very long ago that I went to the market square one day.—
I wore an old German cap which I wore because I didn't have anything else to put on my head. As soon as I got to the square a mumber
of Poles called the militia, who came, tore the cap from my head,
cut it into pieces and put me in jail. Today things are different. They'll
never cut up my cap again! By the way, later on I made quite a row
about my cap,—and you know what? They had to buy me a new one.

"Oh yes, things have improved. And nowadays they leave us Germans
in peace most of the time. Of course, if you walk down the street
in Allenstein or in one of the other cities, and you speak German,
it can still happen to you that a Pole yells "german pig" at you. But
now you can turn around and yell back "polish pig", and you don't
go to jail for it. But, you know,—after a while one has enough,
improvements or no improvements. There's no getting ahead. One
can't hire people to work on the farm, one can't buy agricultural
implements.—Take one of these miserable polish tractors, the "Ursus",
—it costs 60,000 Zloty! That's nothing more than a silly joke. We
haven't a ghost's chance to see that much money all our lives!
"I am just able to get by. And that only because I can do extra work:
I still have a few machines from pre-war days, with which I can do
some jobs for my neigbours,—thrashing and things like that. But
anything new is so expensive that it's almost out of the question. For
instance, I had a new power line laid to my house not long ago; it
should have cost about four thousand Zloty, but it cost eight thousand.
And we could only do it because my wife makes a sort of schnapps
at home. We gave the liquor to the workmen, they got drunk, and so
we had our power line!
"Oh, I can tell you,—that's the way it is all over. With half a litre
of booze you can buy all of Poland. That's why agriculture in the
whole country is going to the dogs. You only have to drive away from
the main roads,—then you can see what the fields look like: fallow
land wherever you look, everything fallow! And only because of
carelessness and burocratic nonsense!

"The burocracy, that's something around here, I tell you. And on top of that the police,—they're the worst gang. I have a relative who works in a government office which is responsible for the distribution of foodstuffs. They had three robberies in that office and its warehouses. In one case they stole a whole lorry load of fresh eggs; and the police doesn't do a thing about it.

"In another case one gang broke into one of these cooperative banks and took 70,000 Zloty. The robbers have never been caught. But one day the militia arrived and deposited 40,000 Zloty into the general funds of this bank without saying a word. No explanations. Nobody knows what really took place. We happen to know one chap who is in the militia and he tells us some of the things that go on. It's best not to repeat them.

"Still, it must be admitted that lately they are making an effort to clean up a bit. A while ago they picked up three militiamen here. Yes, one must say, since Gomulka things have improved. But you know,—he can't be everywhere at once. And, what's more, he himself is sitting right here ... on the tip of a thumb." And with an appropriate gesture he sought to indicate Gomulka's exposed political position.

These remarks soon lead us to a general discussion of the political situation in Poland and particularly in the former german territories under polish administration. The logical sequel was an exposition of this remarkably well-informed farmer's ideas about future political developments. While it was true that life was somewhat improved, even for that small band of Germans who had managed to survive in these parts, he added gloomily:

"If something were to happen here, we Germans would again be the losers."

He was less concerned about polish persecution than russian invasion, and even if nothing drastic were to happen in this area at once, there seemed little purpose in thinking of a real, positive future. "Not right now anyway, perhaps never again."

Soon this third conversation with the farmer had to come to an end, for once again people passed by, whom he did not trust. So we said good bye.

"Next time we'll meet in the West," he called out to us as he swung himself onto his bicycle.

"EITHER FOOD OR CLOTHING ..."

Lötzen.—Our rest period in Lyck was almost entirely used to bring our diaries up to date. Then we had to push on; we are haunted by the fear that we will have insufficient time to complete our big tour; trips in communist countries are always limited by dated visas and extensions are hard to get. However, the days are mercifully long now, as polish summer-time has recently begun and we have gained an hour.

On leaving Lyck we used a road which is not marked on our polish map, and headed for Lötzen. After a while we reached a small village, which was called *Grabnick* in german times. As usual, being away from a main highway and a major city, this village has suffered less war damage. But here too the houses are in a poor state of repair. A small protestant church is intact. It is evident that the church was once surrounded by a cemetary; but the gravestones have all vanished. In front of the church I found an undamaged german war memorial dating from the first world war. The names of the fallen soldiers had been covered with whitewash; but this must have been done in the first years after 1945, and as the general practice of repairing little or nothing applies here too, the whitewash is peeling off and the names of the german soldiers have reappeared.

Jacqueline had remained in the car, while I took photographs. Among those surrounding her was a man who wanted to tell her something, but could only speak Polish. Unable to find anyone among those present who could help him out, many gestures were used to explain, that we should not leave before someone was fetched, who could speak another language.

A messenger was sent off, and as I returned to the car he was speeding back, accompanied by a man who could manage a few words of German and English. He told us the following: the man who wanted to talk to Jacqueline had a brother in Canada. On returning there,—it was naturally assumed that he and we lived in the same city—would we please seek out the polish immigrant and tell him that his brother in Grabnick was well? We promised to do our best, and could now continue on our journey.—Shortly after Grabnick we passed what must have been a very large farm with an adjoining distillery. Bushes and trees grew out of the buildings, and a hare ran from the remains of the stable when I approached to take pictures. The place was deserted. We could not help wondering why such a farm—it could almost be called an estate—had been destroyed; otherwise there had been no signs of war in this district. Why, above all, had the buildings not been reconstructed in order that they might play their part in a country so urgently in need of increased agricultural production?

The next village was once called *Neuhoff*. It was the dirtiest and most neglected community we have seen thus far. Trees, bushes and weeds, —all wild plant life,—thrive here, while the works of man,—be they fields or buildings,—rot and crumble. It is a long time since someone cleaned or tidied up anywhere, and to make matters worse, whatever has collapsed, is left to rot further where it has fallen. The people have adapted themselves to their surroundings; we have rarely seen so many dirty children.

In nearby villages it was the same, and between the communities we saw fallow fields.

Several people, besides the dining room manager in Allenstein, had told us about *Lötzen* (now Gizycko), its beauty and picturesque location on the shore of one of the loveliest lakes in East Prussia. When we arrived our disappointment was great. The entire center of Lötzen is little more than a mass of ruins and hardly any reconstruction work is in progress. Wherever we stopped people gathered. There were many soldiers in the crowd.

First we made a tour of the town. In the eastern part we found more buildings which had survived the holocaust; near the Löwentin Lake several factories were in operation. Tourist facilities, about which we had been told, were nowhere to be found, yet somewhere in the neighbourhood there had to be boarding houses, because we had seen photographs of them.

Lötzen is not large, and we soon returned to the center of the town. We found the Hotel "Miejski" which had been praised so much by the manager in Allenstein. It looked anything but inviting, but since we still planned to go north to Angerburg, and the drive from there back to Allenstein would be very long, we decided at least to look the place over. Jacqueline took on the job. I wanted to make use of the precious daylight hours, parked the car and went off on a photographic tour.

The ruins of Lötzen were depressing, but also dramatically photogenic: at the end of an almost totally shattered wall, which will surely collapse completely in the near future, I found a twisted wrought iron shield, showing a black horse,—probably once the sign of an inn. After taking a number of such shots and looking in vain for a more cheerful subject, I returned to the car.

Jacqueline had just come back from her inspection tour. Her grimly determined words: "Go on, let's get out of here!" told me what I needed to know: the hotel "Miejski" would not be our shelter for the coming night. We drove to a quiter place on the edge of town and Jacqueline jotted down her impressions of the hotel:

Inspection of supposedly charming Hotel "Miejski" shortest I have ever undertaken: roughly ten steps in, ten steps out. This burdensome journey entailed meeting per-step-average of three drunks, three cubic feet of vile smells, three tons of filth. No one paid attention to me, so was able to reach conclusions without trouble: dirt and customers in public rooms without doubt suggest equal amounts of dirt and other mementos of customers in bedrooms. Decided that even if proportion were ten to one in favour of rooms, whole set-up would still be unbearable. After hard days of work we don't have to torture ourselves this way. Long drive to Allenstein certainly preferable.

Retreat from hotel hall to blessed fresh air caused no more stir than arrival. Some drunks blinked, evil-smelling air flowed about me, filth likewise. Au revoir, Hotel "Miejski",—no, à jamais!
Crowd around the car had meanwhile grown so large, did not even try to get through alone. While standing and waiting for Charles, was addressed in German by a young couple. Again german Masurians. Herewith fuller record of our conversation:
They were newly married and so completely without hope as I have rarely found young people to be. The young man told me that he was a mason and earned a thousand Zloty a month.
"If you've been in Poland a few days," he said, "then you'll know that even a man alone can hardly live on a thousand a month."
Therefore his wife worked as a telephone operator and earned an additional nine hundred Zloty a month.
»Although we both work," the man said, "we face the same decision almost every month. What should we buy: either food or clothing?" He showed me his wife's raincoat and his own which was of heavier material. One had cost a thousand Zloty, the other three thousand.
"It's such a treat to be able to speak German," the young woman told me. "Until recently it was forbidden and we could only speak our language secretly. I have seen that you have a canadian plate on your car. I feel a special and personal tie to Canada: about a year ago my father heard a polish short wave broadcast from Canada. Somebody caught him listening and went to the militia and denounced him. My father was put in jail for two weeks. When he was let out, he said it had been worth while. 'We have nothing else with which to pay for what we need; so we have to pay with our freedom,' my father told us at the time. Today things are not that bad anymore. But we want to get out just the same."
"So you're planning to emigrate?" I asked.
"Yes, we've planned to go for a long time, but we have no opportunity," the young man replied. "We have no relatives in Germany and without relatives there is no way of getting out."
"We have no hope of ever getting anything or anywhere," the wife

added. "The fact that we've been able to talk to you today, that's a treat which will brighten our lives for a long time."

Charles returned. I shook hands with the couple. If it were only possible to help such people! Pity is cheap.

Angerburg.—From here to that part of the Soviet border which crosses East Prussia from east to west, it's only another nine miles. We've just driven a short distance towards the border, but since we came upon more and more soldiers and military installations, we soon stopped and returned to this small town which is now called Wegorzewo. In present-day Poland there are relatively few places and things which a cameraman and reporter may not see and photograph, but military installations are, not surprisingly, among the exceptions. We don't want to change the hitherto most tolerant attitude of the authorities by some thoughtless action.

It's certainly evident that the military establishment of the Peoples' Republic of Poland, a nation of 27 million people, is considerable. In the border areas, even along the frontier with the supposed ally, the Soviet Union, the size of this establishment is particularly noticable. Some Poles with whom we discussed this—among them Communist Party members—complained that Poland's armed forces are far too expensive, adding that, should there be another war, Poland would probably be decimated anyway.

On the other hand one could frequently hear a justification of Poland's military build-up: quite apart from a possible war involving the major powers it is necessary, so one is told, for Poland to be able to defend herself in minor skirmishes or limited wars. In the light of history it is not astonishing that Poland fears both East and West, both Germany and Russia. Hence the nation's determination—and this is not only limited to communists—to maintain strong armed forces, to hold on at all costs to the newly secured german territories and to co-operate in all political manoevers designed to stand in the way of german reunification.

Here, in these frontier districts, the fear of Russia becomes doubly

42

evident. Whether and how Poland's armed forces could hold out against a soviet invasion, is another question. But in any case, the very existence of their own forces, commanded once more by polish officers since Gomulka took over, gives the Poles a certain feeling of security,—even if this means a large and frequently criticized budget. And this longing for security plays an important role in determining the political atmosphere of present-day Poland, serving in part to explain the broad basis of public support by which Gomulka rules.

Angerburg, this town near the frontier, is anything but cheerful. Once again the center of town, particularly that part which looks to have been the market place, lies in ruins. The church is virtually undamaged, but around it hardly a single house has remained. As far as could be ascertained, no reconstruction work has been undertaken here to date. It is noticeable that the rubble heaps consist chiefly of stones; it may be that Angerburg was one of those towns which had to deliver a particularly large quantity of bricks to Warsaw, at the time, some years earlier, when all polish or polish-occupied towns had to supply a quota of bricks for the reconstruction of the capital. Of course this can hardly be the only reason for the lack of rebuilding, as bricks and other building materials have meanwhile ceased to be in such short supply. It would seem that this outlying community has simply been ignored even more than others in East Prussia,—either by design, due to the proximity of the border, or because of the continuing transportation crisis which has well-neigh crippled large sections of Poland for years.
Dusk is approaching. We are about to head back to Allenstein.

CITIZEN, FIFTH CLASS

Allenstein.—After our experiences in Lötzen we have now decided to make the Hotel "Warminski" our permanent headquarters while travelling through East Prussia and its western subdivision, West

Prussia. At least we know this hotel and can be reasonably sure that there won't be any unpleasant surprises at the end of long and fatiguing days. However, a certain element of surprise is never lacking hereabouts. For instance, the people one sees in the hotel restaurant. On the evening of our return from Lötzen we observed one group there, which we are not likely to forget soon; every member would have fitted into the script of a third-rate Hollywood gangster film. The "treatment" for such a film would have read as follows:

Into a restaurant filled to the brim with smoke and people, enter The Rat, a short, pale man with a nervous tick in his face. He stands near the door, "cases the joint" with shifty slit-eyed glances, then gestures to some others behind him. Thereupon enter: The Mouse, an even smaller, more nervous type; The Fist, a giant, who looks as if he'd unhesitatingly make mincemeat of everything and everyone, if whoever is his boss were to give a sign. The last to enter is The Creep, a long, thin fellow, who, despite his shape seems to be very agile and clearly spends his time creeping where others fear to tread.

Led by The Rat, the four wander casually into the restaurant, threading their way through the crowd. No table is vacant. They walk up to a table near the dance floor and surround it, that is, each man stands at one of its corners, slowly, meaningfully, crosses his arms and stares pitilessly at the three young people sitting there. All the while The Rat's tick distorts his face at regular intervals, The Mouse whistles an unmelodious tune through his yellow teeth, The Fist thoughtfully rubs his unshaven, square chin, and The Creep gives out intermittant groans, as if creeping through particularly difficult ground at this moment. The scene continues without change for about three minutes; then the three young people get up, showing considerable emotional upset, call for a waiter, who arrives with unusual alacrity, pay their bill and depart. The Rat & Co. immediately occupy the vacant table.

They have no sooner sat down, than enter, accompanied by two additional sinister looking fellows, a young and unusually good looking gipsy. His dark-skinned face has arresting features, his eyes are large, black and flashing. His black, curly hair has been skilfully barbered so as to appear naturally tousled. He wears suede shoes, grey flannel trousers, an expensive looking and perfectly cut brown sports jacket over a light blue polo sweater, and wound twice around his neck, its ends hanging down over his back, a canary-yellow woolen scarf.

As the gipsy and his two companions reach the table occupied by the Rat & Co., the four get up, fetch three more chairs and only sit down again after the gipsy has permitted them to do so with a regal gesture.

Meanwhile dancing continues near the table of the seven. The orchestra plays a form of boogie-woogie; that is, not so much the orchestra as each of the six musicians, who, unconcered by his colleagues, plays his own version. The customers also dance their own private versions, though a common denominator is frequently apparent: most couples clutch each others' upper arms ferociously and then proceed to leap up and down, more or less to the beat of the six musical individualists. These exercises involve a good deal of groaning and sweating, the latter function contributing to some considerable extend to the olfactory delights of the room. Doors and windows of the restaurant being firmly shut, the overwhelmingly scented atmosphere and the shortage of oxygen soon leave their mark on all present: faces tend to become extremely pale and eyes develop a glassy stare. One exception to this general condition is noticable: the gipsy and his six vassals. They seem to be totally unaffected by their surroundings.

The absolute ruler of the six appears far removed from the plebean goings-on around him, even cool, despite the polo sweater, the sports jacket and the scarf. He sits, elbows resting lightly on the table, fingers locked effeminately below his chin, three of his underlings on his right and three on his left. It is now possible to note that his fingernails are very long and carefully manicured. He listens calmly while his creatures talk in urgent whispers; that is to say, all except The Fist, who says nothing whatsoever, restricting his activities to enthusiastic nods whenever the gipsy replies in short, clipped sentences to something he has been asked.

It would seem that the others make a number of suggestions, which the chief either accepts or rejects and, on occasion simply ignores. During this, each vassal displays his characteristics very clearly: it soon becomes evident that The Rat would leave the ship at the slightest provocation, that The Mouse would show considerable skill in extracting the cheese from a well-set trap, that The Creep would have no trouble creeping through any emergency. The two body-guards with which the gipsy arrived, appear to be sturdy types, with extensive experience in the use of knives and small-bore artillery. In fact, an observer soon feels sure that the suggestions made to the gipsy frequently involve the use of such hardware.

During the course of the discussion, vodka and beer are consumed. Then, at a sign from the gipsy, The Rat pays the bill. Abruptly the conversation comes to an end and the gipsy delivers himself of a few precise closing words. Thereupon the others look glum, reach into their trouser pockets and give the gipsy something. A closer look indicates that the "something" is money. The gipsy does not even bother to count the bills, but pockets them with practiced casualness. Now the group silently finished drinks and cigarettes. It is to be noted that the gipsy does this with studied elegance of movement, while the others do not drink but suck in the liquid like defective sinks, nor do they smoke, but puff like steam engines; their cigarettes dangle from their mouths while the ashes drop on their already immensely dirty clothes.

Suddenly the gipsy gets up. The others rise with him. He shakes hands with the four who had arrived first, and, followed by his body-guards, leaves the restaurant. The four sit down again, remain at their table for a short while, then somehow melt into the crowd and vanish.

Soon their table is occupied again by others, who drink vodka and jump up and down while the boogie-woogie music roars and squeals. Compared to all but one of the previous occupants of this table, the new arrivals look like most elegant gentlemen from London's West-end.

The dining room manager was off duty on the day the gipsy and his companions appeared. The following morning he was again on hand to greet us and help us buy the day's supplies for our mid-day meal. Thus I had an opportunity to describe the seven men to him and to ask him whether he knew them. He either did not know or did not want to talk about the six sinister cohorts, but I had no sooner mentioned the gipsy than he said:

"Oh yes, gipsy is known to me. Is, how you say,—very good pants cutter. Cuts fine pants."

I was unable to extract any further information from him.

We are about to continue our travels through East and West Prussia.

Osterode.—On the way to this town which is now called Ostroda, we saw an example of a process which has elicited frequent complaints by the Polish press and causes western visitors to shake their heads in amazement: the collapse of the industrial potential of the former german territories.

There can be no doubt that factories in most parts of this area suffered severe damage during the war. Also, a considerable amount of equipment, indeed sometimes whole machine shops, were disassembled during the first post-war years and taken elsewhere. Nonetheless it is known—and this has been admitted by Warsaw in recent times—that sufficient installations remained more or less intact to have permitted the rehabilitation of quite a few factories. However, the majority of these shops were kept shut down and as time goes by, superannuation, decay and plunder combine to render them useless. Just before Osterode we saw a factory which had been condemned to this form of slow death. It was impossible to find out what had been produced there, but it had evidently been a large concern. We had been able to make out the huge chimney from some distance off and as we approached, we saw what must have been large assembly halls, warehouses and other buildings. We stopped and I entered the factory-compound on foot. I found no trace of bomb damage or other serious scars of war; even most of the windows were whole. But everything was securely locked and weeds and bushes had grown up around the buildings. The small cars of a narrow-gauge factory railway lay here and there, just as they had been tipped over years ago when somebody had taken away the rails. There was a crane too, but without steel hawsers. Wherever I looked I saw the same picture: everything was there,—only not quite complete.

As we were about to drive on, we looked back once more and now discovered three workers: they had a wheel barrow, a shovel and a pick and were removing a heap of gravel from the entrance of one of the buildings. They were taking their time. Otherwise there was no sign of life anywhere.

In Osterode we first made our way to a place which probably used to be the center of town. To our right lay a wooded hillock, to our left a smaller rise on which stood a catholic church and a number of houses. But in the actual center (our Baedecker told us that we had found the right place) everything was destroyed and even most of the rubble had been removed. We could still make out the roofless ruin of a church and a few walls and a broken chimney of what might have been a small factory.

A woman passed us and I accosted her in German. A reporter certainly needs as much luck as good sense. I was lucky. The woman did not only speak the language, she was a German. First of all she only told me that the ruin of the church near us had been the protestant church of Oesterode. Then she turned and evidently wanted to continue on her way; I could tell that she was frightened, uneasy about speaking German with a stranger in a public place. She was dressed poorly, rather like a peasant woman from some outlying village: high boots, black stockings and a grey kerchief knotted below her chin.

I told her who we were, that there was no need for concern and asked her to chat with us a while longer. Although the law against speaking German in public has been withdrawn and despite the fact that we were alone in this desert of a former town center, the woman first looked carefully all around her before she consented to stay and talk to us.

All the buildings which had stood on the empty lots nearby, she said, had been set on fire by the Russians. And with the buildings the lives of the people had been burned down, she thought. It turned out that she was by no means a peasant woman from far away, but the widow of a once-prosperous shop owner.

"Now everything has gone,—everything," she said and made the impression of being less sad than totally resigned. Her voice had no life, no coloring, its tone was completely apathetic.

"Everything has vanished," she murmured, "even the church, which belonged to us all. Only one thing is left to us now, and that is the cemetery. And even this bit of land is no longer as it should be. We few Germans cannot maintain it properly. But we are doing all we can, —because it is almost our last posession, the German cemetery with the fine trees! Once it was beautiful, really beautiful; people came from far and wide to see the flowers and the lawns and the trees. Now it is no longer so beautiful,—but at least we still have our ground. Otherwise,—otherwise everything is destroyed, yes, everything."

The woman shook her head and without another word she wandered away, aimless it seemed, as if she herself were part of the destruction of which she had spoken.

We drove on and searched for the cemetary. After a while we found it, located on top of the hillock we had seen on our arrival. The road leading to it was barely passable although it had clearly been a broad thoroughfare years ago.

While Jacqueline worked on our diaries, I walked through the cemetary and took some photographs.

The trees are really beautiful, so are the plants which thrive so much, that they have overgrown many a grave. Numerous last resting places have virtually vanished and occasionally only the tops of large gravestones are visible in a green sea of ferns and weeds. Then again there are well kept graves. It's easy to tell that some of these have had no attention for some time, but they are surrounded by big stones and wrought iron fences so that allpowerful nature has so far failed to win a victory. Other graves are evidently cared for and decorated with flowers; probably the work of relatives or friends who are still in the district. Here and there new graves have been dug and marked with simple wooden crosses. The names are Polish, or at least half Polish. I wondered if these were cases of voluntary or enforced "polinization": in some instances, the first syllables of the names are German and Polish endings, like "-owski" and "-owa", appear to have been added.

Later we drove through the less damaged part of Osterode. It was hard to believe this lonely provincial community, shabby and deserted, was a city of 18,000 inhabitants not so many years ago. Then we continued, heading south and west.

Deutsch-Eylau.—This is another community in which one needs imagination and reliable documents to believe that 14,000 people once lived here. Now called Ilawa, this town also has a totally destroyed center; in the outskirts people live in houses which are in every possible stage of decay and collapse. A little further outside there is the usual belt of badly kept farm houses—once the market-gardening region for the town—and beyond them the mosaic of cultivated fields and fallow land.

We crossed a bridge which spans a narrow bay of the Geserich Lake and stopped for a short rest in the shade of some large trees standing around a monument of which only the base remains. There we made the acquaintance of the "citizen, fifth class!"

He came towards us while we studied our road maps. I heard his loud footsteps on the paved road, looked up and there he stood, about six feet away: he was very tall, well built though somewhat bent forward, with black hair and a narrow mustache. His face was lean, his cheekbones prominent. He might have been fifty years old, perhaps older. Now he stepped towards me and laid his hands on the ledge of the open car window; these hands were accustomed to physical labour. "Well, for heaven's sake, how did you come here?" he exclaimed in German, obviously assuming that we spoke the language. "What would people like you want in these parts?"

He had a deep voice, and now he roared with laughter. But his face did not show the faintest trace of amusement. I left the car and we sat down on a fallen tree which lay in the former park around the remains of the monument. We lit cigarettes and after I had explained a little about us he told me a great deal about himself.

It was the story of a Masurian who considered himself completely German. He was quite ready to admit that since the first world war there had been many Masurians who could not make up their minds whether they were, as he put it "fish or fowl", whether they should call themselves Germans or Poles.

"I never had any trouble this way," he continued. "And you know, I did not make my decision for nationalistic reasons, but simply because I asked myself: who are you? how do you live? what is foreign to you and what is close to your heart? And soon I knew that in spite of the fact that we have frequently been called Slavs, I had closer social and cultural ties to the Germans. I had been brought up that way, and had always felt that way, so I didn't have to search my soul too deply. Today I am fiftysix years old. Been to university, and lived well, once upon a time, as East Prussian representative of a number of large German companies. Travelled quite a lot too—and saw my share of things. Read a fair amount. Today I have nothing, absolutely nothing, and have to work as a common labourer, just in order to survive.

"Actually I wouldn't mind such a change of fortune, you know.

Happens. But what disturbs me, what grinds me down, is the facts that we, who speak German, who still have our ties with German culture, have become citizens fifth class! That's tough, especially for us, because we know what it is to live properly. Today we don't live any more, we simply exist. Despite all the improvements of late, we are still only granted a bare existence, and no more. In a way this fact isn't astonishing, you know, because, if you think of it, apart from the big shots,—how do the citizens first class have to live? Not much better! You can't imagine what you can see here in the way of burocracy, neglect and waste, simply because no one wants to assume responsibility for anything!

"Oh yes, I'll tell you, in the past years we've had to pu up with a lot. But you only realize how much you can stand when you have to go on, when there's no way out."

I asked, why he hadn't tried to emigrate.

"Tried!" he exclaimed. "God, I've not only tried, I'd walk from here to Germany right now, this minute, just as I am, in my overalls! But they won't let me."

I mentioned the people who had already gone to Germany, the many who were about to go.

"Oh well," the man replied, "if you have relatives outside, then it's not too difficult; but you have to have them,—and quite a bit of luck, otherwise it's out of the question. And that won't change, not for us Masurians. They want to keep as many of us here as possible. And why? Simple! Without us they'd lose every vestige of a politico-legal claim to this land. They need us. They must be able to say: 'the Masurians are Slavs and therefore their land belongs to Poland!' They must be able to prove everything, because what they call 'legality' is one of their fetishes. So the theory runs like this: 'whatever is Prussian in East Prussia, is only a thin upper layer, which was forced on a basically slav land. All that has to go, must be forgotten. Then historical legality will have been reestablished!' That's the way they think."

I mentioned the fact that at one time during the ideological battle over the claim to this region the slav origin of the autochtones had been questioned by Warsaw. My voluble informant brushes this aside with a depreciatory gesture.

"That was just one of those phases," he said and took a deep drag at his cigarette. "One of their theorists tried a new path, but then it was abandoned again. My God, how many times has the world known this artificial game involving historical legality! The communists didn't invent it, and they won't be the last to use it. And still it never works. Why? Because people refuse to see history, justice and the social sciences the way the politicians or their hired scientific yes-men do.

"Most of us here never thought about these things as thoroughly as all that. Some moved away when it was still possible, others stayed here and became what we call Paper-Poles,—they were polonized. Still others had to stay here, for one reason or another, and they had to keep their mouths shut; and this last kind, if they didn't go along with every twist and turn of the game and cheer whatever was served up, they were appointed citizens fifth class.

"Oh, I could tell you a lot about injustice and neglect around here, in big and small things. But you won't be interested in all that. Let's just say that I ask myself how long we will have to stand by and look at this mess."

With that the man shook my hand, returned to the car, bade farewell to Jacqueline and walked away with the same determined steps with which he had approached us.

Throughout our conversation he had not seemed excessively emotional; nor had our presence and the opportunity to speak his mind freely apparently induced him to become unreasonable in his approach to his subject. Only his anger had been evident, the fury of a man, whose mind has been trained to observe what goes on around him and to strive for factual conclusions. Nor did he expect pity, but rather an understanding for a general situation in which he had learned to recognize his own condition as an inseparable part of the whole.

Nonetheless after this man had left us and before we continued on our way, Jacqueline and I decided to review the implications of what he had told me:

We must not forget that we are all too easily recognizable as foreigners from the west. We are travelling through an area in which a most radical political and social change was enforced a relatively short time ago. The change is so recent that there are still many people here, who identify themselves,—their origin, their intellectual roots,— with that part of the world from which we quite obviously come and to which we will return (nationality has become secondary in this connection, only world-parts count). Naturally enough, these people who could be called "the left-overs" from an abruptly ended past, feel themselves particularly drawn to us and, taking advantage of the newly introduced liberalization, which gives them greater freedom of speech, they make use of a rare opportunity and pour out their troubles to us. And if such partners in conversation have also had enough educational background to be able to make an intellectual assessment of their problems, then they are able to draw a vivid— though not necessarily completely balanced—picture for us, highlighting every political error committed during the momentous change-over which has taken place here.

It is clear enough that the economic situation in the part of the former German territories, which we have visited to date, is most critical and that Warsaw will have to do a great deal before even a modicum of improvement can be registered. On the other hand, we, the visitors from the west, with our magnetic attraction for the dissatisfied and for the racial minorities, we must not forget that there may be others here who are quite satisfied with their lot. This may especially apply to new settlers who were brought here after experiencing conditions far worse than anything to be found in this area, and have had a chance to begin life afresh. It is not so easy for us to make contact with such people; and even if we succeeded in reaching them, it would be far more difficult to talk to them openly and to comprehend their thoughts and emotions.

Additional consideration must be given to the abyss which today divides the two remaining parts of the world which are of any geo-political significance. Apart from the disenchanted and the dissatisfied there is only a certain highly trained type of communist who dares to cross the abyss and express in the presence of a non-communist critical opinions about conditions in his country. One hardly ever meets members of such an intellectual elite on a reporting trip through a People's Republic; in Poland certainly not outside Warsaw and a few other centers. This means: most communists—and that includes the Gomulka-communists, who, despite their nationalism are nonetheless marxists—avoid journalist-visitors from the west, unless they have been detailed to keep us company; they do so, either because they are so deeply convinced marxists that they consider all discussion with a casual visitor superfluous, or because they lack sufficient training to know to what extent they can discuss political questions with us and admit obvious errors committed by the system.

Western observers have frequently reported that there are very few really convinced communists in these territories, and probably in the whole of Poland. This may well be true. Certainly a dividing-line is to be drawn between card-carrying party members and ideologically convinced believers. But on the other hand every observer from the west who travels through this country, is bound to reach conclusions on the basis of more or less subjective observations and experiences and hence is exposed to the same pitfalls as we, in trying to assess the political climate correctly. The fact that Gomulka is able to count on so much support in his country, could be an indication that it's not always so easy to draw that dividing line between card-carriers and believers. It may be that a form of communism has found a place in the political thinking of more Poles than some western observers are willing to admit. Some credence may be lent to this theory by the fact, that Gomulka's national communism seems to have worked out a "modus vivendi" with the roman catholic church of Poland.
After a detailed discussion, Jacqueline and I decided to keep these

problems uppermost in our minds while attempting to evaluate future experiences. Every hour of this journey brings so many depressing and negative impressions and the people one meets provide so much intellectually or emotionally overwhelming evidence, that one's judgement could easily be impaired.

THE FEAST OF LIBERATION IN THE RUINS

In a catholic church between Deutsch-Eylau and Rosenberg in West Prussia, a wedding was in progress. As we stopped, the first wedding guests were just beginning to leave the church. It was pleasant to note that about twenty horse-drawn carriages—and not one car—waited outside the church. The guests took their seats, the young bridal pair appeared and mounted the lead-carriage and after a short while, the clergyman hurried out of the church to join them. During this pause the horses—most of them beautiful animals—had become increasingly nervous, and when the priest was finally seated, the carriages rushed off, enveloped in a cloud of dust. This sudden charge almost became a disaster for us.

The horses drawing the third carriage were apparently even less accustomed to an automobile than the others; the presence of our car surprised them so much that they shied and reared. This delay caused the fourth carriage to come dangerously close to the third, and the driver of the former tried desperately to pass on the opposite side of the road from where we were parked; he managed to do this, by a matter of inches, but only after he had slowed down a great deal. Meanwhile the fifth carriage was approaching at break-neck speed and its driver could find no further space to avoid the two others who were blocking the road, nor did he seem to have the presence of mind to bring his vehicle to a stop; instead he simply headed straight for us and tried to squeeze his carriage through the far too narrow space between our car and the shying horses nearest to us. Since I had turned off the motor in order to be able to photograph the wedding from the car without disturbing vibrations, I could not even attempt an evasive manoeuver but sat helplessly, watching the charge. Fortunately the resulting collision affected the other carriage more than us, but still the entire side of the car was scraped considerably. For a moment chaos reigned supreme: the snorting and neighing of the horses, the screams of the wedding guests, thick clouds of dust and loud cracks of whips. In all this not one of the drivers made any attempt to calm his horses—to the contrary: they all yelled and whipped,—trying to achieve greater speed; meanwhile other carriages had come along as well and there appeared to be no end to the consequences which might evolve. Recalling the event now, I still have the feeling of having been on a brief but violent visit to the Wild West of another century. Then suddenly, as quickly as it had developed, the mêlée of horses and carriages was separated and the entire host rushed away. Fortunately the damage is not severe—not too high a price for a short flashback visit to the age before the horseless carriage.

In *Rosenberg,* the beautiful fourteenth century parish church has either suffered little damage or been repaired with great care. The latter may have happened, as it is known that buildings, which date from the seventeenth century and earlier and have historic value, enjoy considerable priority in the reconstruction programmes of most districts in this territory. We have been able to learn this from a number of Polish historical and architectural publications and gather that the reason for this policy may be the absence of typical German characteristics in the building style of that period.

Otherwise Rosenberg, now called Susz, presents a most depressing picture. West of the church, towards the next town, Riesenburg, no houses are left standing and even streets are becoming a jungle of bushes and weeds.

It is extraordinary how different can be the fortunes of two neighbouring towns.

Rosenberg is in ruins. *Riesenburg,* now renamed Prabuty, which lies a mere six miles further west, is in relatively good condition. The same can be reported about the next larger community, *Marienwerder* (Kwidzyn), a large part of which, particularly the business district, is undamaged. On the other hand, a tour through the town did not give us the impression that it still has the population of 20,000 of pre-war times. The famed cathedral and adjoining chapter house have been saved from damage,—miraculously so, for the greatest destruction is to be found in the area immediately around these buildings. Here hardly a house is left. It then occured to us if this was not again a case of priority-rebuilding; both the cathedral and the castle-like chapter house date from the fourteenth century. If reconstruction work was undertaken it was very well done. Meanwhile, the historically less important structures all about are either far down on the list of future projects or may never arise again.

Kurzebrack (Korzeniewo) is a tiny village, west of Marienwerder, which was once East Prussia's only point of contact with the river Weichsel—or Vistula. Today even this minor function has ceased.
As we arrived, the whole village seemed to be soundly asleep. A lonely ferry and its crew of three old men waited in vain for passengers. No one wants to cross the river nowadays. Where to? And so the village slumbers on, unaware of all sounds save the wonderful concert of birds who sing and flutter near the water, and the deep thump of the engines of many river craft which ply frequently between Warsaw and Danzig.

Marienburg (Malbork).—Old books speak of the castle of Marienburg and its surrounding buildings as the most impressive example of medieval architecture in these north-eastern parts. This was once the chapter house and headquarters of the Deutschritterorden, a religious order of knights, which contributed greatly to the civilization and christianization of this region. Unfortunately one has to use photographs in order to see what fine architectural monuments once stood here, for there is little left of the old splendour.

Herewith a transcript of my first impression as recorded on tape, just after we had arrived at Marienburg:
I am facing the castle, having driven across the river Nogat, to get a total view. I have a number of pre-war photographs of the whole group of buildings before me and am going to see how much is still left, or at least recognizable. It isn't much, I fear.
The two round watch towers which—seen from this shore—are to the left of the castle, are intact. Then, further to the right, it begins to look bad. The famous main castle, which includes the palace of the Order's Grand Master, is still standing but damaged severely. Further to the right, there is the so-called "Hochschloss", the high castle. It has been damaged even more. The steeple of St. Mary's church, which belonged to the castle, has disappeared and the upper portion of the "Hochschloss" facade has also gone. Of the fine patrician residences around the market square, which adjoined the castle, nothing remains, other than the ruins of the city hall. The St. Mary's arch, which led from the town to the market square, is half destroyed. The entire opposite shore line, the castle and the oldest part of the town, look from here like nothing more than a depressing grey-black heap of stones.
We are now going to drive back across the river in order to have a closer look at the ruins. End of the tape recording.
Equipped with my cameras and tape recorder I thereupon wandered through the large castle area, in order to record the impressions of the moment and to take pictures at the same time. The transcript:

I've just passed through the St. Mary's arch, and am now in a place which was probably the market square. I say "probably" because I have few real terms of reference by which to orientate myself. Nothing has remained here, except the partially destroyed city hall which I mentioned before. To the left of me, the cellar of a former building: it has an entrance and a roof; this roof was once the ground floor of the building. Above it, nothing,—just rubble. Then over there, a piece of wall, with half an arch in it,—the entrance arch of a building maybe, or one of those arcades which, so the old photographs tell me, decorated the entire market square. A sheep over there, grazing among the ruins. It looks up, stares at me: who are you? it seems to ask. Two men are at work around the halfstanding city hall. They have a shovel and a pick. It's not clear what they are doing. Not much anyway. A third man is asleep near them. The way in which he lies, his twisted face and his open mouth tell an obvious story: vodka.

Nearer to the castle there is another church. It is the catholic parish church which used to mark the northern end of the market square. It has been repaired recently, I can see that. There is fresh white paint on the window frames. A service is going on inside. I can hear organ music and singing. Outside a few men are working on a flower bed which surrounds a statue of the Holy Virgin. This little bit of Marienburg looks remarkably well kept.

Under way again. Walking along the castle's moat, and around the corner. Now I can see how severely the "Hochschloss" has been damaged. I am able to look into the nave of St. Mary's church; not only the steeple is missing,—which I could see from the other side of the river,—but also the entire roof. I can make out a single workman up there; I say "up", because the whole former church is raised above the roadway around the castle. This man will have to do a lot of work before these buildings show any signs of reconstruction. Further towards the main castle there are even more ruins, more halfstanding shells of buildings, and again grazing sheep.

Here and there I see people who are digging in the ruins. Do they still hope to find treasures? Or is it merely a hunt for bricks? Probably that's what they want,—even bricks are precious here. This is surely a sad ruin of a monument to the middle ages, a period in history which is otherwise accorded a place of honor in Poland. Not here. Back to the car. End of the tape recording.

When I returned to Jacqueline, I was greeted by a smiling face and found the following diary entry:

Reporter-husband has interesting experiences with camera and tape-recorder. Reporter-wife also has her share of experiences, occasionally as magnet for people who want to say something, occasionally also as magnet for sinister police types. The latter happened just now. Chronologically as follows:

Am sitting in car. On the horizon,—that is, in front of a large and undamaged building,—appears a single man. Militiaman in blue-grey uniform. He stares straight ahead. I stare straight ahead. Collective staring!

Policeman is very smart. Stares straight ahead, but also manages to inspect car and me. Thinks I can't tell. Mustn't spoil his fun. Militia brain seems hard at work; signs of concentration obvious. Staring is surest sign. Am certain concentration involves development of sinister plan, in which car and I play leading roles. Plan-developing evidently very hard work, for policeman still concentrating. What can I do? Same thing: sit and stare too.

Then little girl, maybe six or seven years old, carrying large shopping bag, comes wandering down street. Girl plans to pass policeman. Nothing doing. Policeman has message for girl. Policeman becomes really cunning: while speaking to girl he turns his back on me. Very subtle! Mustn't show he's talking to girl. Obviously, quite obviously, conversation with girl has nothing whatsoever to do with me!

Conversation over. Girl continues on her way. Now carries shopping bag in one hand, and,—fancy that now—little blue-grey notebook in other hand. Who will be the owner of that book? Answer to this knotty problem soon at hand: girl comes to me, grins shyly. Gives me notebook in which there is a pencil. Girl speaks Polish, which complicates means of communication. But all is well! One word easily recognizable: "autograf"—she wants my autograph! Girl recites whatever she has to say like piece of homework well learned. Very well learned,—but maybe a little recently. In any case, my reaction negative. Explain to girl, am not famous,—"zadem autograf".

Girl smiles, though clearly shaken. Takes back notebook. Great future for girl as detective or other subtle operative: returns straight to

policeman, who has resumed staring position. Again highly successful
secret activity: police back is turned, conversation with girl resumed.
Marvellous solution to entire problem found! Suspicious foreigner
will undoubtedly tumble into newly invented trap!
Girl returns to me. Grins again, recites fresh homework containing
word "autograph".
Must not disappoint poor child. Take notebook and pencil and give
autograph: "Sherlock Holmes, Canada."
Girl runs back to policeman, smiling with delight. Both now wander
down street, away from me.
Am happy to have contributed to general enlightenment of Polish
militia.
Charles is coming up the street. Does he want "autograf" too?

On my return from the castle I found a booklet—rather like a
theater programme—lying in the street. On the little page there was
a photograph of the Castle of Marienburg; it did not look exactly
as it was in former times, nor the way it looks today; a certain
amount of retouching had been done. Under the picture was written:
"8.-9. Czerwca, 1457-1957" and under it a short text. With the help
of our dictionary we found out that on the occasion of the five
hundredth anniversary of the "liberation" of Malbork a "Feast of
Liberation" was to take place. The programme for this feast contained
a good deal about the "history" and "fortunes" of the castle: the
"liberation" of 1457 was described as an immensely important event
in Polish history. The programme promised a celebration which was
to include tours of the castle, presentations of historical plays, folk
music and dancing, a concert by the "Baltic Philharmonic Orchestra"
and a number of sports events.
In order not to give Jacqueline's militia-friend another opportunity
for an autograph hunt, we've moved to a spot outside Marienburg,
where we have combined a small meal with our programme-decypher-
ing session. We can't help wondering what this event will be like,
back there, behind us,—the Feast of Liberation in the Ruins.

We are now going to leave the main road and drive back to Allenstein in a round-about way, in order to see some of the outlying countryside.

POTEMKIAN FIELDS

En route across West Prussia.—For a while we drove back along the main road to Marienwerder. In the village of Stuhm (Sztum) we turned east and continued along a narrow side road.

After a short drive through a forest we came upon an estate which once was surely magnificent. It was still possible to imagine what it must have been like: surrounded by fine fields and splendid farm buildings, a charming small chateau, set in a well kept garden and ringed by ancient, tall trees.

Now the fields are in unbelievably neglected condition. It's still possible to tell that the earth is fertile. Even the way in which the fields were once planned indicated a profound knowledge of efficient agricultural methods.

The stables and barns are already beginning to collapse, a process which has started because the roofs have been allowed to decay. A sign on the former chateau indicates that this is now a "P.G.R.", a state farm. Part of a herd of black-and-white cattle grazes on a nearby meadow, the rest in the former chateau garden. On the broad terrace of the chateau there stand a number of cows. Many sows and piglets roll about in deep mud which is to be found on all paths and roads. In a field between the chateau and the stables several agricultural implements, ploughs, hoes and the like, are parked and look as if they had not been used for a long time: rust has made them all but useless. Geese wander over the roads and chicken hunt for food in the former garden. Very few people are to be seen. A man is asleep beside the entrance to a stable, two women stand on the chateau terrace and seem to have nothing to do. A child tends the cattle on the meadow.

A few minutes later we reached a second estate which, according to a sign over its entrance, had become a collective farm. There the situation was equally bad. Next to the neglected old buildings, wooden huts had been put up; they were unpainted, small, with perhaps one or two rooms, and though obviously quite recently built, already showing signs of decay. There were many people about, wading up to their knees in the deep mud puddles around the huts. A large pack of mongrel dogs charged our car and barked hysterically. We drove on, through extensive fields which could only belong to the collective, and were remained of what the peasant in Lyck had told us about agricultural conditions away from the major highways: ploughed land alternated with at least as many acres which had lain fallow so long, that they resembled a steppe. Moreover, on examining the fields on which crops were growing, we made an astonishing discovery. Jacqueline, who has more opportunities to look around while I drive, was the first to become aware of something strange. "I could be mistaken," she said, "but the wheat here and the rye over there isn't going to feed many people."

I stopped, left the car and saw what she meant: the grain had been sowed only along the edges of these fields, in strips which were no more than nine feet wide! In the middle the land lay fallow. Sometimes the sowed strip didn't even surround the entire field, but ran only parallel with the road.

We soon had a name for what we had found: Potemkian Fields. In this case, the Czarina Catherine, for whom these dummy fields had been prepared was no doubt an important burocrat or politician from Warsaw.

Why? we asked ourselves. What was to be gained by such a show? Mere laziness could hardly be the reason, as it would not be much more work to plant an entire field. There seemed to be only two possible explanations:

Either: the crop delivery-quota set for the farm in question, was too great to be fulfilled. Hence a smaller acreage was sowed, but in such a manner as not to become noticeable during a casual inspection. At harvest time, when deliveries had to be made, it would then be necessary to invent an excuse, but probably whoever was responsible hoped that "post factum" the punishment would not be severe.

Or: there was a shortage of seed grain. When dealing with the buro-cratic hierarchy of a totalitarian state, such shortages can rarely be admitted, let alone discussed. Therefore the managers of collectives or state farms, and even private farmers with too burdensome a delivery quota, might well prefer to use the dummy sowing method in order to protect themselves from the controlling officials as long as possible.

After some experience with an agricultural system managed by a buro-cracy, one can well imagine the thought-process: it is preferable, the lowest rank of officialdom thinks, to present superiors with a "fait accompli" than to draw their attention to problems at an early stage; thus it is possible to avoid,—or at least postpone,—a lot of trouble and additional work for which there is little or no incentive in the form of extra pay. Hence: Potemkian Fields.

Christburg—now Dzierzgon—has a severely damaged central area. A water-tower atop the castle hill, which has always been considered a landmark, is still visible, but a city-square and surrounding streets at the foot of the hill, have vanished.

There were no traffic shields signs in the town. Since so many roads are not marked on our maps (even the German one is not as complete as it might be), it was once again necessary to navigate by instinct. But in Christburg this was not a reliable means of choosing from among two or three possible routes and before we had left the town far behind, we found some shields which made us realize that we had taken a wrong turn. Soon we were back at the foot of the castle hill. Although we could ill afford a loss of time, the error had its advant-age: we were able to have a closer look at an east Prussian town removed from the main highways.

In the narrow streets away from the destroyed center of Christburg, a thought which had come to us before recurred: neither air raids nor heavy artillery bombardments alone were responsible for the metamorphosis which has taken place in these territories in so short a span of time. The presence of a new population sometimes would appear to be more important in giving houses, streets, even an entire town a stamp, an all-enveloping atmosphere, which tells of indifference, neglect and finally,—desolation. It was late in the afternoon; we looked at the people who sat before their houses, staring at us with almost total passivity,—at us and yet at nothing, for we felt sure that their expressions would have been the same had we not passed. It seemed that we had come upon a form of destruction just as frightful as there, where the buildings are ruins and the streets filled with rubble.

After touring the town for a while, we drove away in a southerly direction and, at Alt-Christburg, turned once more towards the east.

Saalfeld-in-East Prussia has been renamed Zalewo. When a road sign announced the beginning of the community, we could not believe our eyes. Where was the little town? We could only find a handful of half-shattered houses and nothing else. We drove on, past the houses and up a small hill. There we saw where Saalfeld must have stood.

We discovered the ruin of a church, recognizeable only by the shards of a half-shattered entrance which stood amidst fallen walls. The square which probably surrounded the church had disappeared, save the cobble-stones; of buildings, only a few withered foundations remained. In the distance we made out three structures which could still be called houses. These were inhabited. Beyond them the emptiness continued. It was possible to make out a few former streets, but only after a search through a thick cover of weeds and bushes; once stone steps led from there to what used to be private gardens. Today the steps lead to nothing. This is a ghost town in every sense of the word. It was getting late; dusk had fallen. As we stood and stared, something startled Jacqueline:

"For heaven's sake, look over there!" she whispered, pointing between two particularly eerie-looking ruins.

A quick glance and I was no less surprised. There was a skull over there—huge and weird! It looked like the skull of some primeval monster, with enormous white bones. But—between these white forms there were also black shapes which, now that we looked carefully, seemed to be more than mere shadows. Then the whole thing moved, —moved and advanced towards us. It was a black-and-white cow, with markings on her head which resembled a skull. Slowly she approached, her lean body swaying from side to side as she carefully picked her way among the treacherous rubble. Hastily we moved away and had soon fled the ghost town.

Mohrungen (Morag).—The blue-grey light of dusk continues for a long time up here in the north; it has a merciful way of enveloping everything—ruins, decay and desolation,—in a mantle which obscures the most depressing aspects. This town, the birth-place of the famous eighteenth century German philosopher and writer Johann Gottfried von Herder, was wrapped in such a gauze-like cover and seemed more pleasant at first glance, before a closer look revealed the truth: here too there were ruins, poverty and all the signs of squalid existence.

In a room on the ground-floor of a small house along our road a light was burning,—a single bulb which hung forlornly from the ceiling. "This is the way people live here," Jacqueline said.

We stopped and looked into the room:

Bare, yellowish walls, from which the whitewash had long peeled off. An old cupboard, made of plywood or perhaps cardboard. Next to it a large wickerwork trunk, which was being used us a sideboard. Two camp beds and an old chair. In the center of the room, a wooden case and on it a bottle of vodka. Three men and two women sat on the beds and the chair. Somewhere outside our field of vision children played and yelled. Dense clouds of smoke filled the air. Somebody reached for the bottle of vodka, drank and handed it around. The electric bulb swayed from side to side,—probably because someone was walking on the floor above. One of the five looked out and saw us. The window was closed and a horse-blanket hung across it,—over one of its panes; the other was broken.

In vain we searched for the house in which Herder was born. Twice we asked for directions but were not understood; the name Herder meant nothing. It may be that the house has gone, or that it is no longer marked as the birthplace of a famous German; perhaps, had we had daylight and time to search further, we might have found what we sought. But even as we groped through the darkness our activities came to a sudden halt:

A reddish light blinked at us from a short distance down the road. The light was so feeble that I nearly ran over it and the man who held it. That would have been a major disaster, for it was a militiaman, waving a flash-light.

I managed to stop at the last moment. The policeman came to my window, saluted and rattled off a long sentence in polish, of which I failed to understand anything but a single word: "dokumenty".

Police check-points are no rarity in Poland, particularly in the evening hours. A few years ago these controls took place at the entrances and exits of all larger towns. Now they are becoming a little less numerous; we had not been stopped once since our arrival in Warsaw. A few evenings ago a control just outside Allenstein had turned out to be only for vehicles with Polish licenses: we had been waved on.

In this case I wasn't sure if we had come to a control point for all vehicles, or if we were being checked because of our all-too obvious search for the Herder house. In the latter case, it was easy to imagine a situation in which,—if we were unlucky—my cameras and tape recorder could be confiscated, the car impounded and we might become involved in an endless interview at the nearest militia headquarters. Whatever the consequence would really be, I felt myself becoming nervous.

I produced our passports, opened them at the page containing our Polish visas and handed them to the policeman. The officer began to read; it was a lengthy process, protracted the more because he soon turned to the other pages and studied old and long-cancelled Polish permits. When I tried to explain by means of many gestures, that the rest of the book could be of no interest to him and again pointed to our current visas, he only shook his head and resumed leafing through every page of the passports. After a while, a second militiaman appeared out of the shadows and began looking over his colleague's shoulder.

My nervousness combined with an impatience to get back to Allenstein and I made the mistake of betraying my feelings to the officers. Jacqueline whispered a warning and I made a determined effort to hold myself in check. But it was evidently too late; the policemen now gave me to understand that they were not satisfied with our passports alone and wanted to see other documents. They were not rude, but made their demands very clear.

My irritation increased. Despite the danger of annoying the two officers, my only thought was that I did not wish to sit there another hour while they read all our documents. So I played dumb, shrugged my soulders and stared uncomprehendingly.

"Perhaps they only want the documents for the car," Jacqueline whispered.

I did not accept her suggestion, although I somehow felt that it might be wise. But nervousness had quickly developed into stubborness and I could not seem to dislodge myself from the uncomprehending position I had assumed. Now, having thought the situation over I realize how close we came to serious difficulties. But fortunately we were lucky this time.

For a while the two policemen debated. Then they again studied our passports and once more tried to explain or demand something, whereupon I looked as vacant as before. At last they closed our passports with a determined (or was it resigned?) snap, handed them back to me, saluted smartly and let us go.

We drove for about ten minutes, then stopped to revive ourselves with the aid of a cup of coffee and to discuss the incident. We agreed that I had not acted wisely and would have to use different tactics, should the occasion arise again.

About fifteen miles further, we once more saw a small red light. This time it didn't take long: I opened the glove compartment and pulled out all the documents I could reach: those pertaining to insurance receipts and policies, international motor vehicle permits and driver's licenses, as well as a few old tickets for an Austrian alpine road and a receipt for freight charges covering the shipment of the car through a tunnel in Switzerland. I was just about to produce our passports as well, when the militiamen saluted and the control was over.

There is always something new to learn!

MARKETING DAY AMONG THE UKRANIANS

Guttstadt.—The German name of this town suggests the words "good town". When the polish administration re-baptized the towns, the meaning of Guttstadt's name was maintained and it is now called Dobre Miasto.

We arrived here in the morning of an unusually fine day. At first we thought: this is one of the exceptions, the town seems quite well kept. We had arrived from the south, and the first streets of Guttstadt were undamaged. Above the roofs in the distance, we could see the steeple of the medieval catholic parish church. We had high hopes of being able to find an undamaged center of town as well. But we were soon disappointed.

All the houses around the church have vanished, although the church itself has once again escaped major damage. (Here too the possibility exists that repairs were undertaken, since the structure dates from the fourteenth century.) Elsewhere nothing has been rebuild. Storks had nested on the roof of an ancient tower; otherwise few inhabitants were to be seen.

While I took photographs, about ten men with—I thought—noticeably slav features, appeared from nowhere and stood around me. I asked if one of them spoke German. All but one shook their heads. The latter was by no means fluent, but managed to tell me that Guttstadt had been the victim of a revenge action by the Soviet Army, and had been systematically burned down. The reason: at the end of the war, the German commanding officer had been a native of Guttstadt and a holder of the "Ritterkreuz", the German Wehrmacht's highest award. He had held the town as long as it was possible,—longer than necessary, my Polish informant thought—and when he was finally forced to retreat, the Soviets revenged themselves.

No one can say that today this town is a "dobre miasto"—a "good town".

We have now stopped for a short rest on the highway to Heilsberg and have taken the opportunity to bring our diary entries up to date. Above us jet fighters are streaking across the deepblue sky, engines howling, canon stuttering. We've heard their target practice almost since leaving Allenstein this morning.

Oh dear! here comes a motorcycle with side car, carrying three militia-men. Are we due for another control? In broad daylight? That would be something new. Indeed,—they are stopping.

Yes, that was it. It took seven minutes this time. One of the three officers spoke excellent French. I had to explain who we are, why we are parked here and what all our documents meant. In this case it was no use playing dumb or showing old toll tickets and the like. The French-speaking officer was extremely polite, almost friendly, and thanked us for the information we gave him. It may be that,— without realizing it,—we have crossed into a restricted area. The jets overhead emphasize this possibility. In any case, the police made remarkably few difficults, but they certainly were full of curiosity.

Heilsberg.—It is Tuesday, Marketing Day, and the activity in this town, renamed Lidzbark Warminski, is positively overwhelming! Beginning at the very outskirts of town the streets are filled to over-flowing with horse-drawn carts, on which rides a shouting, gesticulating and vodka-drinking multitude. Near the market it is even more crowded, with hundreds of people milling around the open stalls of a typical Polish rag-fair.

Up to now our experiences here have been brief, but exciting.

By keeping my hand on the car's horn and driving at a snail's pace, I managed to get us to the middle of town. There we again found much damage to the buildings, although the impressive old castle, a fortress which belonged to the Deutschritterorden, the religious knights, is well kept.

Heilsberg was once an important center for the Ermländer, a group of "autochthones" related to the Masurians. We failed to discover any trace of these inhabitants. For the first time during our travels in these parts I could not make contact with anyone who spoke German. Then I remembered a rumour, which I had heard in Warsaw, that several thousand Ukranians had been settled hereabouts some time ago. Our findings seemed to confirm this.

I left the car in Jacqueline's care—here it seemed ill-advised to leave it unguarded—and walked through the crowd, in order to get close-up pictures of the stalls, the buyers and sellers at the rag-fair. I soon felt as if I were somewhere in western Russia: the market was the same sort of pitiful exhibition, featuring trivial merchandize of the poorest quality as one sees on photographs of Russian provincial towns; above all, the people would have fitted perfectly into such a setting: by their physiognomy, behaviour and dress they seemed far less European than all other new settlers we had hitherto seen in this territory. Then too, the people displayed much more temperament,— even to the way they surrounded, touched and rocked our car (rocking being the most popular method of "testing" western cars in all east European countries) and to the way the women hid their faces and ran, screaming, from me as soon as they saw my cameras. Then there was the soldier, who kept slapping me on the shoulder, screaming "Kamerad!" into my ear, and gesticulating wildly to make me understand that he insisted on having his picture taken. On the other hand, two other soldiers, who had seen me taken pictures, marched up to me, tried to confiscate my cameras and arrest me. By chance I still had in my pocket a very impressive-looking invitation- and admission-card to a performance of the "Mazowsche" Folk Music Ensemble in Warsaw. I showed the card with its gold print to the two soldiers. They let go of me at once, shook my hand and marched on. Nonetheless, the tumult and the thought that Jacqueline was alone, made me uneasy.

Returning to the car, I was just in time to prevent a fist-fight. A young gipsy woman in long skirts and a man in overalls were yelling at each other, ready to resort to violence. A sizeable crowd had collected around them, cheering one or the other would-be combattant. I gave myself a push, used my arms like a wind-mill, shouted and flailed my way through the spectators; then with more desperation than courage I rushed on, between gipsy woman and man in overalls, reached the car door, tore it open, leaped in and started the engine. With my hand firmly on the horn and my foot pushing the accelerator to the floor I managed to make the quickest start of my life.

While I weaved in and out among the farm carts, Jacqueline told me that the gipsy woman had leaned into the car through the open window, had asked for money and, seeing that none was forthcoming, had then begun to finger several camera lenses which lay on the seat. Jacqueline had tried to get rid of the woman, but without success. Thereupon the man had arrived, had pulled the woman out of the window and in no time the argument had been on.

It seemed that the man in overalls had felt himself destined to become Jacqueline's protector. While he had gone into action to realize this ambition, the object of his protective instincts had not needed a profound knowledge of Polish to gather what the voluble conversation outside the car was about. It had begun by not very complimentary references to the parentage and manner of birth of both protagonists, and had soon shifted to observations regarding Jacqueline's virtue which, the protector had seemed to maintain, was being besmirched by the woman's very presence. The while Jacqueline had felt that, had the protector won the fist-fight, he would have considered it part

73

of the victor's rightful spoils to continue where his defeated enemy had left off.

"I had the distinct impression," Jacqueline observed, "that he would not only have leaned through the window, but would have entered the car as well. He might even have tried to drive off with me, if you hadn't come back in time. Who knows, by now I might be on my way to the Ukraine or some place like that!"

I should record here that such incidents have their compensations: it's quite pleasant, for a change, to be regarded not only as husband, but as knight errant and saviour. But not too often. The risks for all concerned is a little too great.

In order to write down the details of our experiences with the wild citizens of Heilsberg, we have halted again. We are parked before the old city gate and both of us are busy with our notes. But already another screaming mass of people has gathered around us. Fortunately our notes are complete.

"Please go on," Jacqueline has just said. She has had enough. So have I. We are off, heading north-west, to the Baltic sea coast and Brauensberg.

On the road.—The road to Braunsberg is very poor and is rarely used by cars or trucks. But we have seen many horsedrawn carts and noted that the animals were well kept and of a race which, despite heavy, muscular bodies, has the slim legs of race horses. These are probably "Trakehner", the remnants of a once-famous east Prussian breed.

In Mehlsack—now Pieniezno—we passed a state tractor station. Agricultural machines of all kinds stood in the open air and rust had spread over most of them. But the public address system, which blared military band music throughout the big station, was in excellent condition. The music was deafening.

Ploskinia was probably once the village of Peterswalde. In the case of small communities it is not always easy to find the former German name. Shortly after the village, we once again passed acres of fallow fields where nothing has been planted for years and farm houses which cause one to wonder how people can possibly live in them without attempting to make at least the most urgent repairs. Every part of these houses is desintegrating. The windows are broken and covered by paper, the doors are held shut by nails, because the hinges are missing. While taking photographs, we were able to ascertain, that frequently several families share accomodations under one roof. One can tell by the dirty washing hung up outside the broken windows, by the numerous ancient baby carriages, which are left around the houses and by the many children of the same age, which are everywhere.

Braunsberg (Braniewo).—Shortly before reaching this town near the Baltic coast, we passed over a bridge and stopped in order to look for the river which it spanned. Instead, we found a concrete highway, with a badly cracked surface, from which sprouted patches of grass. It was the "Autobahn" connecting the one-time capital of East Prussia, Königsberg, (now in Soviet territory) with the city of Elbing in West Prussia, it was some day to have gone through to Berlin.

We stopped, took photographs and spent about half an hour on the bridge. Not a single vehicle passed beneath us. Although there was a sign on the road leading from the bridge down to the big highway which read "Na Autostradzie"—"to the Autobahn",—the same sign also provided the additional information: "Przejazdu niema", "no thoroughfare". Evidently bridges or whole sections of the Autobahn are out of commission. Above all, a few miles north of here begins the Soviet zone of East Prussia, which is totally sealed off. It's a wonder the whole highway hasn't disappeared under a blanket of grass. But it probably won't be long now.

At the city limits of Braunsberg there was again a militiaman who wanted "dokumenty". This time the officer was only interested in our passports, which he read through from cover to cover. Then he took one of the documents, walked slowly to the front of the car and compared our license with the number of the passport. At first the fact that the numbers did not match seemed to disturb him. Then he nodded wisely, and the control was over.

After a short drive through streets with more or less undamaged houses, we again came into a desert. Beyond this large area, in which everything had been flattened, stood a skyline of heavily damaged buildings; among these, beyond the river Passarge, we could make out the shells of two churches. Another building, which must have been a monastery, was in part destroyed, in part repaired in a haphazard way. Paths, which may once have been streets, threaded their way through the heaps of rubble; on these we saw some horse-carts. Otherwise there was hardly a sign of life.

Frauenberg.—Little more than the famous fourteenth century cathedral has remained of this town. Copernicus is burried in the cathedral and a memorial tower to the astronomer stands on a hillock above the church; the latter is not entirely preserved: its upper portion is missing and a small tree has taken root on top of it.

At the foot of the memorial hill a large noticeboard has been put up, bearing the inscription "Turystyka", and meant for the posting of tourists information. Apart from the cathedral and the memorial there can be nothing in the ruins of Frauenberg—now called Frombork— which might be of any interest to tourists.

While I was taking photographs, a few people approached. They were particularly friendly and suggested repeatedly that I should photograph the "Turystyka" noticeboard.

"That very good for laughing," one man said in halting German, "visit beautiful wrecked town and learn to be happy at home."

"Do you think that it would be good for foreigners to see these sights here?" I asked.

"Yes," the man replied, in a half-serious, half-sarcastic tone of voice. "Ruins are good for morale. Also good for not making war again."

The highway to Elbing is in good condition. This largest west Prussian town before the Danzig area, isn't far off.

Elbing (Elblag).—Only the mechanical eye of a camera can accept and record without horror what is left of the once-proud hanseatic town of Elbing.—The cameraman, who has to hold the camera, must make a determined effort not to shudder, turn away and drive off as quickly as possible.

A verbal report is quickly made: parts of the business and industrial sector of the town are still recognizeable, although badly damaged; here at least some rebuilding or repair has been considered worth while. In the "Altstadt"—the oldest part of the town— nothing has escaped virtually total destruction; this includes the market square, the hanseatic merchants' houses and the "Speicherviertel", a section of famed old houses along the Elbing river. And nothing, absolutely nothing has been done to make repairs or even to clean up the horribly twisted wreckage of the past. While parts of the Nikolai Church can still be made out, the church steeple looks like a frightful skeleton, which reaches far above the ruins. Only one bridge still spans the Elbing river, the others lie in the water, exactly as they fell when the bombs struck them. All around, parts of chimneys, walls and towers reach into the sky,—dreadful memorials to international mass murder.

Here too one sees people who dig in the ruins, seeking whatever this vast graveyard will yield; others wander—aimlessly it seems—through this scene of horror, as lacking in hope as their surroundings.

The walls of some wrecked houses still bear the remains of German inscriptions: "Goldener Löwe" (Golden Lion) "Einbahnstrasse" (one way street) "Bank",—and, all at once, a small bell tinkles! It comes from the barely roofed-over nave of the Nikolai Church. It is the acolyte's bell. A service is in progress in there, amidst the ruins. Prayers are said,—"On earth peace, goodwill towards men . . ."
How urgent is this prayer! How often has man acted against it! How

dreadful a memorial is Elbing, an unhealed wound, to recall what was done in the name of national honour.

In Elbing, in the ruined church, prayers are said, whilest all about lie the shards of a town which was once the second-largest in West-Prussia,—and beyond it there is this West Prussia, indeed the whole of East Prussia, also largely in ruins or fallow. One can only hope that the prayer will help, will be heard,—not only to avoid a repetition of the events which caused this horror, but also that this land might find a worthy future. Whoever may govern here from now on, no matter what political beliefs he may hold, will surely have to recognize, that the conditions which prevail here today, cannot, must not be permitted to continue. The prayer must help. But deeds must follow.

At the former german-polish border near Neidenburg in East Prussia. A shield now marks another border there: the one between the provinces of Allenstein (Olsztyn) and Warsaw. Here our journey through the former german territories under polish administration began. Several weeks and 4,000 miles later we left the territories near Hindenburg in Silesia.

WARSAW. The first day of our tour began in the polish capital. In the background the Hotel »Bristol«, surrounded by a scaffold. In the foreground our car; here it did not attract so much attention. Later it was to be quite different.

GILGENBURG. Only one row of houses was still standing on the market square of this little town in East Prussia. We were not used to so much destruction and could hardly believe our eyes.

THE TANNENBERG MEMORIAL, as it once looked.

And this is the way it looks today: the memorial is completely destroyed, the park around it has become a wilderness. A polish peasant grazes his goat near the shattered memorial to Hindenburg's first world war victory over the Russians.

The walls of the Tannenberg memorial were blown up at Hitler's orders. In some places the brickwork still stands in the rubble.

The center of the memorial looks like an gigantic crater. In it, a single recognizable memento: the remains of a large statue of Field-Marshall Hindenburg.

ALLENSTEIN. View from the Copernicus Tower at the castle. As a provincial capital, the town has more inhabitants than in 1939. The center of the town was damaged during the war but the ruins have been cleared away. Some of the best known buildings have been renovated, as for instance the »New City Hall« (steeple at extreme left). A city gate, the »Hohe Tor«, is on the right.

The center of Allenstein near the arch of the »Hohe Tor«. In the background, the steeple of the protestant church.

The courtyard of the Allenstein castle. The building is well preserved and used as a museum. In the foreground the Copernicus Clock.

Since Gomulka there is more religious freedom in Poland. In an old street of Allenstein we found this recently opened shop for religious articles.

BISCHOFSBURG. The center of the town is severely damaged but the market square is being repaved and some houses are under repair.

On our way we frequently saw fallow land. Sometimes the fields were turning into steppe. Sometimes — as here, between Bischofsburg and Sensburg — one could still see that the fields had been ploughed until some time ago.

SENSBURG is the cultural center of the remaining protestant Masurians. The town made a gloomy impression. As usual there was no vehicular traffic, except for one old cart. Here we met a young Masurian who told us about the life of his compatriots.

Again and again we saw lilac bushes planted in squares on both sides of the highway. In the middle of the squares, there was nothing but a pile of sand and rubble. These were the remains of houses. This picture was taken between Sensburg and Barranoven.

Near Barranoven we saw the buildings of a collective farm. The houses were shabby and neglected, the cattle fat but dirty. Only the horses looked very well-kept.

BARRANOVEN. This was the first pleasant picture on our journey: the village church surrounded by lilac bushes. Though the building was intact, a closer look revealed that it too had suffered a little: all its windows were broken.

In a little village between Nikolaiken and the eastern town of Lyck we saw the first german inscription. This house was once a cooperative saving's bank named after the founder of the organization. Similar institutions are still found all over Germany today.

Wherever we stopped, a large crowd gathered. First the children came running, but soon the adults followed. In this way we met many people.

LYCK. There are great gaps among the houses in the main street along the lake. In the background, the steeple of the renovated protestant church. It is now used for catholic services.

In front of the church seen in the picture above, all the houses have disappeared. This was once a densely built-up area.

GRABNICK. This german war memorial of the first world war was covered with whitewash by the polish autorities. But since no repairs are made, the whitewash is fading away and the names of the fallen soldiers are reappearing.

Bushes and trees grow out of the smashed buildings of this former farm. A rabbit ran out of the stable on the left when I approached to take this photograph.

LÖTZEN. The center of the town was full of ghostly ruins. Everywhere the remains of the destroyed buildings reached into the sky.

On a battered wall in Lötzen we saw this shield: a black horse, which probably once marked an inn.

ANGERBURG.
Near here the Soviet border crosses East Prussia from east to west. The town has suffered greatly. Its center looks like this. As is so often the case, the church has survived the holocaust.

Among the people who came to our car in Angerburg, we saw typical easter Poles, as for instance this boy.

HEILSBERG. The appearance of the new inhabitants of Heilsberg gave us a clue to their origin: many of them are Ukrainians who were settled here not long ago.

On the market square of Heilsberg two soldiers wanted to arrest me while I photographed. A third called me »Kamerad« and insisted that I take this picture.

GUTTSTADT. When we approached Guttstadt from the south, it looked as if we were coming to a well-preserved town. But our hopes were soon dashed. All that is standing in the center of town is the tower of the medieval catholic parish church.

The rest of Guttstadt looks no better. Entire blocks of houses are missing. The old tower in the background is unharmed and, as during past centuries, storks still nest here.

OSTERODE. Weeds have overgrown many graves in the former german cemetary (above). — Occasionally a gravestone sticks out among the plants and bushes (below). Only a few graves are well-kept.

The castle of Heilsberg, built by the »Deutschritterorden«, a sect of religious knights, is well preserved. But the castle is surrounded by ruins. Farm carts are almost the only vehicles one sees here. Cars are rare.

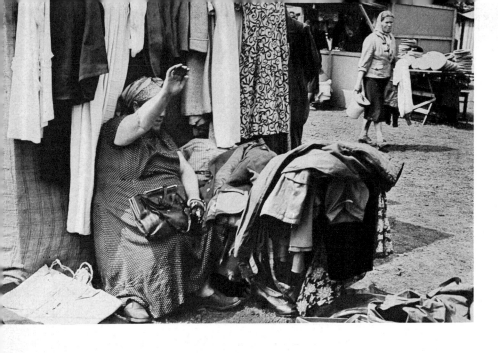

The rag-fair on the »Marktplatz«, the market square, in Heilsberg. It reminded of western Russia and certainly not East Prussia (above). — Near by, food was being sold: a few pounds of vegetables spread on newspapers (below).

MARIENWERDER. Much of this town is undamaged, particularly the business district around this building. It is the local government office. However, driving through the town, we did not have the impression that it had anywhere near as many inhabitants as the 20,000 who lived here in pre-war days.

KURZEBRACK, a little village west of Marienwerder, was once East Prussia's only outlet to the river Vistula. Today it does not even fulfil this function. When we arrived, a lonely ferry waited in vain for passengers.

En route in West Prussia: quite apart from their curiosity, the people whom we met during our journey were very friendly. The eastern Pole in this picture wore a tattered german army uniform and was extremely pleased to be photographed in it.

In the center of Osterode everything has been destroyed. One can barely make out the ruin of a protestant church (above) and the remains of a former factory whose chimney reaches into the sky (below). In the background, the spires of another church, around which some blocks of houses have escaped damage.

On our journey we saw this peasant wedding. The horses were so unaccustomed to cars, that they shied and we narrowly escaped a serious accident.

ROSENBERG-IN-WEST PRUSSIA. The beautiful 14th century church is in good condition. We could not find out whether it escaped war-time damage or had been renovated.

One of the most famous parts of Marienburg's »Hochschloß« or »High Castle«, was the St. Mary's Church. Looking at the castle from across the river it had been apparent that the church steeple was missing; but a walk around the castle revealed how much more serious the damage was.

ELBING. The second world war left little of the town standing. The Nikolai church and the well-known merchants' houses facing the Elbing river (above) have become ghostly skeletons (below). The picture showing the ruins was taken from exactly the same spot as the pre-war picture above.

MARIENBURG.
Above: the famous castle Marienburg has been severely damaged. This does not appear as readily on the picture above, taken from a point across the river Nogat. Below: A pre-war picture taken from the same location; although it looks as if only a few parts of the castle are missing in the picture above, the following pages show the true extent of the damage.

The buildings around the castle have all but vanished. The »Marktplatz«, or market square, which adjoined the castle, consists of nothing but these grotesque ruins (above). Only the catholic church, also located in this area, has been renovated recently (below). In front of the church some people are working on a flower bed surrounding a statue of the Virgin Mary.

FRAUENBURG. The church in which the great astronomer Copernicus is burried is intact, but the Copernicus Tower, seen on this picture, is badly damaged. Little is left of the rest of this town.

BRAUNSBERG. While part of this town is still in existance, the major section, on the southern shore of the river Passarge, consists almost only of ruins. Beyond the buildings shown here we saw two destroyed churches and a partially rebuilt structure which appeared to be a monastery.

Not far from Braunsberg we saw many neglected farm houses, such as the one on this picture. It was sometimes difficult to understand how people could live in these buildings without making any repairs.

North of Braunsberg we crossed over the Autobahn which connects Elbing with the former capital of East Prussia, Königsberg. There was no traffic there. Moreover, a few miles north of here the Autobahn enters the totally sealed-off Soviet part of East Prussia.

Everywhere in the old part of Elbing, portions of chimneys and walls reach into the sky like dreadful memorials to the international mass-murder which is war. The people who wander about here are as cheerless as their surroundings (above). At various places men and women dig among the ruins (below). It is not clear what they seek, treasures, or merely bricks?

Of the »Altstadt«, the oldest part of Elbing, not a single building is still standing
(above). In the years since the war nothing has been cleared away, nothing has been
touched. On various houses one can still find the remains of german inscriptions,
as for instance on the ruin of the inn »Goldener Löwe«, which stood between the
Nikolai Church and the Elbing river (below).

DANZIG
EASTERN POMMERANIA
EAST BRANDENBURG

IN THE WINGS OF A GIANT STAGE

Danzig.—Danzig 1957 is a city of contrasts and contradictions. One sees and hears astonishing things.

The Polish journalist who lives in the former hanseatic- and League of Nations-city declares: "Gdansk is Polish, because it is a historical fact that the city always had close ties with the heart of Poland and because for a long time, it was the outlet towards the sea of the entire Polish hinterland. Gdansk is Polish, because it is situated at the estuary of our greatest river,—the Visla."

One of the few Germans who still lives in Danzig, is told of this statement and replies: "According to this way of thinking, one might just as well say that Hamburg belongs to Czechoslovakia, because it is situated at the mouth of the Elbe."

Seen from a purely political point of view, Danzig today is indeed a Polish city. But the contrasts and contradictions exist nonetheless, and one doesn't have to search long before they become apparent.

We knew that bitter battles at the very end of the war for the possession of the hanseatic city and aerial bombardments had combined to destroy Danzig almost completely. As we drove through the lowlands at the mouth of the Vistula and were nearing the eastern limits of the town, we naturally asked ourselves, to what extent—if any— Danzig would be rebuilt; had the hanseatic town's many churches and world-famous merchants' houses with their gabled roofs and elaborate facades been consigned to oblivion or was a reconstruction programme under way?

Our first glimpse of the town did not provide an answer to our questions. We drove through an industrial suburb, which showed signs of war damage, and where a number of factories and houses had also been rebuilt. But, we told ourselves, industrial suburbs are never typical for a city.

Then we reached a street which, an old city map indicated, was formerly called "Langgarten". Hardly any buildings stood here on either side of the street, although this had been a densely built-up area. The ruins were overgrown with grass. A few minutes later we could see much further ahead, and now faced an astonishing skyline: destroyed buildings in every immaginable stage of collapse and decay, side by side with many others which could only be described as apparently quite undamaged. However, the sun was near the western horizon, and its powerful light made it hard to get a closer look at these strangely preserved buildings; then we reached a bridge, once called the "Milchkannen Brücke", and our panoramic view was obscured. We crossed the bridge and continued on the former "Milchkannen" street, which traverses a small island, the "Speicher Insel". Then followed an undamaged bridge across the river Mottlau, the "Grüne Brücke", from which one enters into the heart of the old city through a city-gate. The gate—once named "Das Grüne Tor"— was also well preserved; we drove through it to reach the old town's one-time main street, the "Lange Markt." Here we stopped and stared in disbelief:

The famous patrician merchants' houses of the "Lange Markt" were all there, showing no signs of damage! Even the city hall, at the far end of the street and the "Artushof", the building in which Hitler once made a rabble-rousing speech, were there, exactly as they appeared on old photographs.

Then, as we began to inspect this astonishing sight with greater care, we noticed that here and there portions of the facades of the houses were incomplete; occasionally a statue was missing in a niche or on the gable of a house; one structure near the Neptune fountain was surrounded by scaffolding. These buildings had not miraculously escaped war-time destruction,—they were new! new and, in fact, still being completed.

It seemed incredible. After days spent in a region in which reconstruction is a great rarity, it was as if we had come into another world. We decided to make sure that we were not mistaken, and drove on towards the city hall, planning to continue from there along the "Lange Gasse", the equally well-known extension of the "Lange Markt". This proved impossible as the "Lange Gasse" was a one-way street, and I had to turn left into a narrow alley, just wide enough to permit the car to pass. As we drove on, our uncertainty came to an end; it was as if one looked into the wings of a vast, excellently constructed stage; only the facades of the merchants' houses had been rebuilt in their original form; behind they were indeed new, all side and rear walls being of bare brick which, unlike the facades, had no coat of mortar. Between the houses facing the "Lange Markt" and another row fronting on the next parallel street there was an open space, which, our Baedecker told us, had not existed before. There building materials and rubble from the original structures lay about. We decided that this was done in an effort to rebuild only those rows of houses needed to reconstruct the most famous old streets of Danzig.

We continued through the narrow alley and reached the former "Hundegasse", the street running parallel to the "Lange Markt". Here we discovered another phase of this astonishing reconstruction programme: the buildings on this street were all practically finished, but the decorations had not yet been added to their front. We saw two rows of brick buildings, the outlines of which corresponded with those of the patrician houses of the sixteenth to eighteenth centuries, but otherwise were modern structures.

The small alley by which we had reached the "Hundegasse" continued a little further and there, all of a sudden, the entire undertaking came to an end as abruptly as it had begun: beyond the houses on the "Hundegasse" there was a vast area of rubble in which not a single building, not a piece of wall was standing; at its far end we recognized the burned-out shell of the St. Petri- and Pauli chuch, the only faintly recognizeable point of reference. Apart from a few men who were loading bricks onto ancient carts, we could not see any signs of life in this sea of stone. Then we remembered that the official working day in Poland was long over: it begins very early in the morning and continues—often without a lunch break—until three in the afternoon. Continuing through the destroyed area, we passed a spot where two wooden shields marked the junction of two small footpaths; these had been streets and would undoubtedly become streets again. The names were now in Polish, but we had no trouble indentifying their location in our Baedecker and hence realized that in this part of the rebuilding programme those in charge were following the original layout exactly.

We returned to the "Hundegasse", drove to the end of the street and, reaching a square once called the "Heumarkt", we tried to find the road to Zopport, the resort near Danzig, where we had reserved a room in the "Orbis"-Grand Hotel.

The old Danzig now lay to our right. We could look down ancient streets, lined by new imitations of the classical buildings. Some were almost finished, others still surrounded by scaffolding. Then there were some of the original buildings, which either had escaped destruction by some miracle, or had been worth repairing. And again the feeling of being in the wings of a giant stage overcame us: we were at a vantage point, which opened to us a vista of contrasts and contradictions. In part we had a view of the "stage", where the magic is performed; in part we could also see into the "wings", where the magic is brewed, where stand the mechanical aids, where the view of how it is all done can be a bitter disappointment and almost like a fraud.

The "stage hands" were missing at this moment, but the "actors" were about, in large, colourful numbers. And these actors,—the inhabitants of Gdansk—helped to create the theater atmosphere and to underscore all the contrasts and contradictions: it was as if the wrong actors had come perform here. The set was german, but the actors could neither speak the german language, nor had they any cultural or ethnic ties to the set, indeed to the entire stage on which they had appeared.

One does not have to look far to realize that culturally and ethnically Danzig is german; this is especially noticable in that part of the town which is being rebuilt by Poland. The marks of german culture never really vanished, not now, not even during the almost three hundred and fifty years, beginning in the second half of the fifteenth century, during which the kings of Poland were the nominal sovereigns of Danzig. The other period in history when the city had no direct ties with german cultural influences—the short period as a "Free City" during the twentieth century—left no mark whatsoever on the basic character of the town. In fact, it was this unfortunate interim attempt at a solution of a profound political and sociological problem which, combined with the undeniable german make-up of Danzig, gave Hitler-Germany an opportunity to create and foster nationalistic agitations, which, in turn, prepared the way to the second world war.

Despite these dreadful events, it would be quite senseless to ignore the German character of this hanseatic port city. Only present-day Poland will not hear of this fact, if one reads the official declarations from Warsaw. Yet, and this seems so contradictory, this same government in Warsaw decided to rebuild the war-destroyed city of Danzig. In doing so, it was impossible to avoid emphasizing the german characteristics.

And to this were added the "wrong actors":

The original inhabitants of Danzig, whose very nature was reflected by the outward appearance of their town, were driven out and new citizens with totally different cultural roots, were ordered to move in and settle down. On the stage, before the brand new but still german setting—made in Poland—stood brand new actors—bought from eastern Poland—and played ... they hardly knew what. Certainly nothing german.

Hence the visitor's impression of looking at a stage is heightened:

everywhere there are the contrasts, contradictions and unrealities which one is only prepared to accept wholly when held spellbound by the magic of the theater. In a city street, this acceptance becomes difficult.

And so we, the reporters from the west, stood on this "stage",—the street in Danzig—, surrounded by a host of "actors"—the new citizens from the east,—and tried to find our way through a labyrinth of new buildings, blocked streets, heaps of rubble and deep craters, in order to reach our hotel in Zoppot. We could find no one who spoke German or any other western language; perhaps this was unusual, perhaps quite typical for the new Gdansk.

At last, by means of gestures and drawings, we managed to orientate ourselves. Continuing, we reached a tree-lined avenue—formerly called "Grosse Allee"—which leads to the once-famous and elegant spa, Zoppot. The avenue was in remarkably good condition,—the first well-kept city street since Warsaw—but the villas, set in large gardens, which line it, were neglected. We then passed a new district of shops and large, monotonous apartment blocks, drove through the suburb of *Olivia,* where few signs of destruction were visible, and then entered *Zoppot.* Once again it was more difficult to get directions than it had been in some of the towns of East Prussia. After losing our way twice, success was at hand: we saw a large yellowish building with an impressive entrance ramp,—and there it was,— the Grand Hotel.

This hotel once ranked among the foremost in Europa. It is completely intact, but is surrounded by grounds and service buildings which are dilapidated. In the hotel, the public rooms, excepting the dining room, have vanished. However a renovation programme was begun in the summer season of 1957, which may lead to considerable improvements. The dining room could be much better too, if it were aired once in a while and if the service were not quite so poor. The state-employed waiter takes his time; tips are coming into fashion again (tipping never really stopped, but was officially frowned upon as "capitalistic"). But this has failed to make an impression on the venerable gentlemen who serve here. Of course there are exceptions, but once a good waiter has been discovered, it's no use trying to sit at one of his tables for more than one or two occasions. The waiters' shifts call for a man to work one day from early morning until late at night, then take the next day off.

As in most old-fashioned hotel buildings, the kitchen at the Grand Hotel in Zoppot is far away from the dining room, and the people who work down there, seem even less interested in efficiency, nor do they receive the occasional tip which might speed up the odd waiter. Hence the kitchen personnel takes life particularly easy and all meals are cold long before they reach the tables. The menu is limited and the shortage of meat, fresh vegetables and fruit is noticable.

Our room is located in a wing of the hotel which has recently been renovated; it's clean here and we do not need to use our own bed linen. We have a private bathroom, with fixtures which are almost of historical value, but everything works. All this, and a splendid view of the sea makes our stay here by far the most pleasant we have had in Poland up to now.

Workers are busy day and night, striving to complete the renovation of the hotel before the main summer seasons begins. This does not make for restful nights—a machine which whines like a neurotic lunatic is being used between midnight and dawn over our heads— but one does have the impression that an effort is being made to eradicate the traces left by years of neglect in the better hotels and to prepare them for some kind of tourism.

THE BRUSH OF CLEANLINESS

Since we have come to Danzig, we have asked ourselves repeatedly, why the Polish state, which, as everyone knows, is in the greatest financial difficulties, is going to the expense of rebuilding Danzig in the old style. In order to find about this, I made contact with the local authorities as soon as possible, and was able to arrange an interview with the chief architect of the Danzig reconstruction programme. We first met Mr. Lech Kadlubowski in a coffee house, then went with him to the office of the Danzig reconstruction architects and completed our talks in his home.

Mr. Kadlubowski, a young and vigorous man, impressed us as being extremely open-minded and completely fascinated by his own immense task. He has at his disposal a vast store of knowledge and background material about the former Danzig. He is a native of Wilna, the eastern polish town which is now part of the Soviet Union, and completed most of his studies in Warsaw. As he told us with regret, he never knew Danzig before its destruction. The staff he directs includes twenty-four architects, twelve sculptors and fifteen painters as well as an army of construction workers.

The reconstruction programme had its practical beginnings in 1949 and is supposed to be completed by 1960. Mr. Kadlubowski seemed confident that this plan would be carried out according to schedule, in as far as it concerns the rebuilding of the old city and the patrician houses; another project, which calls for a completely new part of town, to be located between the old city and the waterfront would take much longer, he predicted.

At his office and in his home, the architect showed us scale models of the entire project—the part to be rebuilt and the new city. The models of the old town had been painstakingly constructed by Mr. Kadlubowski and his assistants, according to photographs, old prints, plans and descriptions in books.

"The preparations took a long time," Mr. Kadlubowski told us, "but now that we are building, everything is going a little too quickly." He spoke German fluently, having also studied at a german university. I asked whether the speed of construction was reflected in the quality of the buildings. The architect nodded. "Unfortunately, yes," he said. We were then told of the considerable difficulties encountered in trying to evolve a cohesive programme out of the opinions and ideas of a total of twenty five architects. The aim was to achieve a fusion

120

of modern town planning and construction, and of the old architectural style of Danzig.

"We want to build classical houses," Mr. Kadlubowski went on, "without forgetting the needs of the people who are to live in them. That is the reason why we have left more space between the rows of houses which face the streets. There we are going to plant trees and lawns."

This explained the empty spaces, filled with rubble and building materials, which we had seen.

It was difficult, the chief architect went on to say, to put modern flats into the narrow classical houses. These had been built at a time when a section of street-frontage, no matter how small, was a valuable possesion; hence the structures had no width, but were very deep. The odd shapes of the flats did not appeal to most new tenants, who preferred modern houses outside the reconstructed old city.

Mr. Kadlubowski told us that of the population of 200,000 in present-day Gdansk (before the war there were 265,000) only a negligible percentage was of german origin. In other words: the German-problem had ceased to exist here. But there were still some autochthones, we were told, particularly those who had been driven out of Danzig a few years ago. They had not left Poland, having preferred to stay in some other part of the country where they were not persecuted. Now they were coming back.

"That was one of the great mistakes of the stalinist era," the architect said. "And now it is our duty to accomodate these people. This is very difficult, because we have no room for them yet."

Mr. Kadlubowski went to great pains to point out that the style of the old Danzig was in no way German, that no German town was being rebuilt here. "The style was very mixed,—Italian, even from India, and above all Dutch," he said.

"German too?" I asked.

"Yes," was the reply, and I thought the architect hesitated a moment. "Yes, that too."

I asked how the eastern Poles fared in this town.

Mr. Kadlubowski shrugged his shoulders. "It's not always good," he said in his extremely frank manner. "You must understand,—those who come from far away, feel this is not their real home. And then you have to add the political question: these people have a great, great fear of war,—and they are not at all convinced that they will always have a secure and permanent home here."

"And will they continue to feel this way?" I asked.

"I don't think so," the architect replied. "The next generation will show great improvements."

After this interview, the "City Reconstruction Planning Commission" arranged a visit to one of the new flats in a rebuilt house.

An official, who was also to be our interpreter, led us to a house in the "Lange Gasse", which had been completed, he told us, less than three years ago. From the outside the building was correct in every detail of style and also gave the impression of being very solid. But inside, the process of decay had already begun. In the very narrow staircase, which had such a low ceiling that a tall man would surely knock his head, the mortar was cracked and falling down and several steps were broken. The flat to which we were being taken belonged to a factory worker. We found the entire family at home: the man, his wife and two children and the wife's mother. They were friendly but understandably embarrassed. We did not have the feeling that this family or the flat had been especially selected as a propaganda show-piece for foreigners.

The flat consisted of a tiny entrance hall, a small living room containing an old day-bed, an equally small bedroom and a kitchen which looked like a narrow passageway. There was a very primitive toilet but no bathroom. The furniture was of poor quality, and in part damaged. The only mirror in the flat was badly cracked. On the chest of drawers in the bedroom, there stood a picture of the Holy Virgin and a crucifix. The walls were bare, save for two cheap coloured prints; where there was wall-paper, it was beginning to peel, while the mortar was breaking off in other places.

I wanted to shoot some television film and, in order to improve the light, had to screw a 500-Watt bulb into one of the fixtures. I had no sooner turned the bulb on, than a crackling sound was heard from the wall, smoke billowed from the light switch and the fixture could not be turned off again; to avoid a short-circuit, I had to take the lighted bulb out of the socket. The woman of the house smiled pleasantly and let me know that there was always trouble with the electric fixtures.

Jacqueline drew my attention to the fact that there were no facilities for hanging up laundry, and we then saw some rather dirty washing which had been hung outside the living room window, where it touched the wall of the building. Jacqueline, always interested in such matters, also noticed the small gas stove in the kitchen, which had only two rings.

There was one expensive article in the midst of all this poverty: a large and evidently new radio with an attached record player. I recalled how often, during our travels through eastern european countries, we had noticed that the poorest people owned elaborate radio sets.

All the rooms of the flat were clean, and it seemed unlikely that a special house-cleaning had been undertaken before our arrival. But even this cleanliness could not really brighten this gloomy home.

Then an object caught my eye: on the kitchen wall there was a cloth container with two brushes. Over the brushes these words were embroidered:

"Wir zwei sind immer bereit
für häusliche Reinlichkeit."

A German rhyme: we two are always prepared for domestic cleanliness!

After we had left the flat, we could not, with the best will, find many words in praise of what we had seen. In order to mention something pleasant Jacqueline and I, almost as if by accord, talked about the one positive impression we had had: the cleanliness of the rooms. Our guide-interpreter's reply was typical of the readiness to admit failings one finds so frequently among Poles and which adds so much to their appeal: "Oh yes, of course," he said and shrugged his shoulders, "it's no wonder the place is like that. The woman is of German descent." And he chuckled to himself.

The day following our inspection of the flat, I asked that we be taken to the office of a Polish newspaper appearing in Danzig, so that we might meet Polish colleagues and discuss life and politics in this town. First we met a woman-editor, a native of Warsaw. She told me she had worked in Danzig—of course she called it Gdansk—since 1947. She declared herself firmly convinced, that Danzig was now a Polish city, and considered it pointless to doubt that this metamorphosis would be permanent. For her there could be no polemics on this subject, she merely made a statement which she considered inalterable. I then asked why the town was being rebuilt as it had been before the war, since it had not been part of Poland, either politically or culturally.

The lady-journalist had a ready answer:

"You must understand, we Poles have lost so many cultural monu‑ ments, that we must preserve and keep the ones we have as best we can and, if necessary, rebuild some of those which were destroyed."

This reply led to another question: how could Poland afford such a luxury, when it was known that there was a desperate housing shortage all over the country? Once more there was a prompt reply.

"I think we have to face the fact that we cannot satisfy everybody, whatever we do. Since we are rebuilding the city in its former style, people say: 'this is an unjustifiable luxury!' If we were to rebuild the town in a modern style, people would cry: 'Criminals! destroyers of culture!' And if we had left everything exactly as it lay when we took over here, then people would have said: 'Of course, the Poles! they never do anything!' We can never do it right for everybody. But still, I think we have found the right way. "

Then we talked to a man who was a member of the paper's manage‑ ment. We had to wait for him, because he was attending a meeting of a communst party committee. He only dealt with Poland's historical and political claim to Danzig. It was he who made the statement, already mentioned, that Danzig's location at the mouth of the Vistula and the city's long-time function as the port of the polish hinterland, made Poland's claim absolutely clear. He also declared that in the years during which Danzig was part of Germany, an artificial "germanization" programme had been carried out and that many Poles had been driven from the town.

"But now we have succeeded in making Gdansk a Polish city once again, and this is the way it will remain," he declared at the end of our interview.

We then went on a further tour of the city. This time the working day was not yet over, and we could see how much was being done. In many different parts of town work was in progress on houses, churches and famous land-marks, including the almost totally destroyed "Krantor", a medieval crane tower.

We watched the arrival of a truck-load of bath tubs in front of a block of flats which was nearing completion. The tubs were rather small and primitive, but nonetheless served to show us that the flat we had visited was not typical of accomodations in all rebuilt houses. St. Mary's church, the largest in Danzig, which was severely damaged at the end of the war, has been completely repaired on the outside; the interior was also about to be finished. In this case, we learnt, an agreement had been made between the state and the church, according to which the former undertook the reconstruction of the building's exterior, while the latter assumed responsibility for the interior.

It was interesting to note that frequently old pieces of buildings were incorporated in the reconstruction. Door frames and entrance arches often survived bombing or fires better than other portions of a house and were the sole surviving parts of an otherwise vanished structure. In the rebuilding of Danzig, these entrance arches are being used again, and whole houses are built around them; at the same time the ornamental masonry which belonged over such entrances and over windows and gables, is also used if it can still be found.

On the "Lange Markt", the most famous of the ancient streets, work has been—as already mentioned—almost completed. The best-known buildings, the "Steffen'sche Haus", the "Schöffen Haus" and the "Artushof" and many others have been replaced, lacking only a few details of ornamentation.

As we visited various building sites, we noticed again and again, how primitive were the available tools and machines. At one place we watched a dozen workers lowering sewage pipes, at least twelve inches in diameter and about thirty feet long into a vertical position in the ground. The only machine they had for this job, was an ancient winch on a tri-pod of wooden support-beams, with a rope that had to be wound by hand. Close by, a number of men worked on a block of eight or ten houses; they had a single, small and ancient cement mixer. Horse-drawn carts brought sand and bricks; there was not a crane or tractor in sight, only a few superannuated trucks. We thought: this was not only a rebuilding of classical forms, but also one with the tools of by-gone days.

As we left the building sites, the working day had already come to an end. We noticed an astonishing number of the workers, who were now on their way home, staggering through the roads and alleys, completely drunk. I pointed this out to our interpreter, who had shown us around the city, adding that driving to the newspaper office early that morning we had seen people just as drunk on their way to work. "Yes, I know, it is terrible," replied the Pole, and showed me an article which had appeared that day in the newspaper we had visited. "Some official statistics have been announced today," he explained, "according to which during the last three months the average monthly income of a Polish family has been spent—among other items—as follows: 67 Zloty for clothing, 127 Zloty for meat, and as the most expensive item, 147 Zloty for alcoholic beverages. An the newspaper goes on to say that unless something is done very soon to fight alcoholism in Poland, drunkenness will shortly become the most serious national problem in our country."

After the interpreter had left us, we continued our drive through the city. We came to a public market in one of the narrow old streets, where fresh fruit and vegetables were on sale. Not having eaten nor even seen anything of the kind for several days, we stopped and bought some shalots, raddishes, and a pound of small, sour and very expensive cherries. We were about to drive on, when I was addressed by a grey-haired man in shabby clothes.

"You're certainly not used to such miserable goods," he said, speaking German without any accent. He looked very tired and his face was sickly-pale.

I nodded, expecting that some bitter words about life in present-day Danzig would follow. I did not have to wait long:

"You should have seen what one could buy here in the olden days," the man continued. "That," he motioned to the market, "is nothing but a bad joke!"

In a slightly sarcastic tone he told me that he was a German, who had been forced to leave Danzig, his home town, in the period immediately after the war. But he had had no relatives abroad, and was thus prevented from leaving Poland.

"And then I suddenly discovered," he went on, "that I really wasn't a German at all, but one of those 'autochthones' as they call it,—a Kaschube,—you know, from what used to be the corridor." And he grinned scornfully. "Well, when they heard about that, they suddenly let me come back. And here I am today,—working as a construction hand."

"What was your profession before?" I asked.

"I had my own business. Quite a jump, isn't it? But that's the way things are in Polish Danzig."

I took the opportunity to tell the man of the Polish journalist and his statement that Poland had a just claim to Danzig, based on historical and practical facts. This caused the former businessman to make the previously quoted remark, that in this case one would have to say that Hamburg belonged to Czechoslovakia. Then he went on:

"There really isn't much point in going on with this debate. In politics, there is only one rule hereabouts, which everyone has to accept: Might is Right. And whatever exists, remains that way until Might forces a change.—I hope you'll enjoy those weeds you've bought there! If ever you should be able to buy something better here, then you'll know that the change has been forced. But that may take a long time!"

He gave me a sort of salute with two fingers, murmured something about having to buy some weeds for himself as well, and went on his way.

We are making preparations for the next part of our trip. We cannot help feeling that Danzig is probably condemned to be a permanent political bone of contention, despite "polonization" or "germanization", claims by all concerned, and reconstruction in the traditional and modern manner. The argument over the posession of this town, which has been going on so long, the unfortunate attempts by the League of Nations to internationalize the city, all this is part of Danzig's apparently inescapable destiny. It is even doubtful whether Poland's massive colonization programme of today will bring about a permanent change, for here the German-Polish conflict is already deeply rooted, while in other formerly German areas it is still in its early stages of development.

THE THREE HUNDRED DOLLAR CARS

Before continuing our journey in a westerly direction, we made a short side-trip to Kartuzy. Between the two world wars, this town was part of the Polish Corridor. Before that the place was called *Karthaus*. We were interested in trying to locate a supposedly sizeable minority group of Kaschubes who were said to live here.

We found a typical Polish provincial town. There was hardly any evidence of war-time damage, and although there were also no signs of prosperity, the over-all impression was at least not as gloomy as it had been in the cities which had been part of Germany more recently.

Shortly after our arrival on the market square of Kartuzy, we were surrounded by a group of from forty to fifty men. When I asked, whether they were all Kaschubes and could therefore surely speak German, most of them remained silent. Only two or three men nodded and began to talk to me. One of them, a man of perhaps forty five years, with black curly hair and a bushy moustache, was really fluent in German, although he had an unusual, slavic-sounding accent. As he stood near the open car window, I turned on my tape recorder and took down the following short conversation:

C. W.: But you speak excellent German.
Kaschube: Oh well, we are all Germans here!
C. W.: So you consider yourselves,—you feel as Germans?
Kaschube: Oh well,—we are Germans or Poles, any way you like it. You know how these things are: at one time this was part of Germany here. Then it was Poland, then it was Germany again,—and now it's Poland once more. It always goes like that here ... like a see-saw.
C. W.: And what do you prefer?
Kaschube: Oh, don't ask things like that. It's better not to ask questions and better still never to answer them. Ask me if I want to have a car like yours. Then I can give you a clear answer. (*Long pause*) But what's the use of talking about cars, when we don't have enough to eat?
C. W.: In other words, life is very hard here?
Kaschube: Oh, wonderful! Absolutely wonderful! *(Dry laughter. Then again pause)* You can't imagine how it is.
C. W.: But you are permitted to speak German now, aren't you?
Kaschube: Yes, they've made the regulations easier now. Five years ago it wasn't like this,—let me tell you. We have a sort of—what they call—freedom, now. *(Again dry laughter)* Well,—good bye!

Conversations with the other men who could speak German were restricted to our car. Polish car manufacturers would take a hundred years to produce a model like ours, one man thought. (It is interesting to note that the span of a hundred years was frequently used when someone spoke of the time it would take for improvements to become really tangible in their daily lives.) The people seemed to have a bitter, disillusioned attitude. Their clothing was very poor.

Gdynia.—From Kartuzy it was a mere twenty miles back to the main highway Danzig-Zoppot-Gdynia. Poland's only sea-port between the two wars, which before the end of the first world war was called Gdingen, and which the Nazis renamed Gotenhafen for a short period, seems to have suffered no war damage. At first we thought that the impression of prosperity, which we gained as soon as we reached Gdynia, stemmed from the fact that we saw no ruins; an uninterrupted row of houses had become an unfamiliar sight. But soon we noticed other signs of economic well-being: there were more goods on sale in the shops than anywhere else in northern Poland.

We were particularly interested to see the varieties of merchandise displayed by the so-called "Delikatesy" shops; these specialty stores also sell some foreign foods, especially canned goods. It had already been explained to us in Warsaw, that the tins reach these shops, because Poles who receive food parcels from friends or relatives abroad prefer to sell to the state some of the things they are sent, in order to get even more urgently needed cash. The prices at which the state then resells the goods is staggering, when one thinks of the average monthly wage of barely 1000 Zloty: a small tin (48 gramms) of instant coffee, 95 Zloty; a normal-sized tin of grapefruit or orange juice, 30 Zloty; a very small tin of lemon juice, 35 Zloty; a tin of peeled tomatoes, a polish export article, 22 Zloty; a half-liter bottle of domestic vodka, so-called "second quality", 38 Zloty.

The clothing stores of Gdynia have much better wares on sale, but the prices are also considerably higher. A nylon blouse we saw cost 546 Zloty; a pair of men's shoes, rather like sandals, 649 Zloty.

Not surprisingly, one sees quite a lot of sailors here. In fact, the traffic in the streets,—both pedestrian and vehicular,— is quite lively. There is an unusually large number of cars, with license-plates which begin with the letter "H"; these identify private cars. Even more astonishing is the fact that many of these cars are of a American manufacture, mostly of the years 1948 to 1953. I tried to find someone who might be able to explain this; but it was not easy, for our car attracted much less attention here than elsewhere. We did not even have the usual crowd around us, from which to select a useful informant. After I had accosted several people in the street without any success, I finally came across a communicative subject. He was a man with a full beard and the swaying walk of a seaman.

"It's this way," he told me and chuckled to himself, "for a long time Polish sailors were permitted to buy and bring home three hundred Dollars' worth of goods every time they left the country. I can't exactly explain how they managed to buy these cars,— perhaps it was slightly illegal, perhaps they were able to save up their three hundred Dollars from several trips abroad. In any case, they brought back the cars on their own ships. And now they either drive them here, or they've managed to sell them for an enormous profit. There are people who are quite ready to pay 100,000 Zloty for a car."

"But who has that much money?" I asked.

"Oh, don't you worry," the man replied, "there are enough people who make big profits! And nowadays they're not even asked where they've made their money."

"And what happens," I inquired, "when one of these cars breaks down and has to be repaired? Can one get service and spare parts?"

"Of course not! There is nothing!" was the prompt answer. "Nothing to be done but to use a bit of string and some wire. And there's not even the slightest hope of getting spare parts by means of newly brought-in cars which might be taken apart, because now the three hundred Dollar car business has come to an end,—no more can come in. But on the other hand, it's always possible to find a way out of trouble, particularly in a port city."

"Where you a sailor yourself some day, or are you still one?" I asked. The man gave me a wily grin. "Let's just say, I've been around quite a bit," he said.

At that moment a young man approached us. He was well-dressed and carried an expensive-looking and evidently brand new briefcase. He addressed me in Polish. I asked my anonymous car-expert to act as interpreter. The man chortled, stroked his beard and translated: "He wants to know for how much you'll sell your car."

I said something about it being a very long walk home without a car, that customs regulations were not to be ignored and that I also wouldn't know what to do with more than a hundred thousand Zloty. Then I thanked the expert for his information and the would-be buyer for his offer, and we continued on our way.

Now, after having taken some pictures of Gdynia, we are heading towards Pomerania, and the first town in that former german province, Lauenburg.

Lauenburg,—renamed Lebork—shows little or no signs of war damage. Only the very center, around the parish church, has been laid low. It may be that Lauenburg was largely saved by the fact that the prewar Polish frontier was located a mere two and a half miles to the east, and that the victorious Soviet armies (which also left Gdynia untouched) did not begin their punishment actions until they were further advanced into german territory. The streets of Lauenburg were filled with pedestrians and again we noticed the eastern, almost Asiatic features and clothing of the people. Compared to Gdynia, the shops are very poor. For the first time,—maybe by chance or because the transportation crisis is particularly severe in this region—we saw cues in front of food stores; this was the case at a milk distribution center, a butchers' and a bakery where large loaves of black bread were on sale. As we looked at these cues, we aroused a good deal of attention and soon enough a militiaman approached. We decided to drive on. We had to find a gasoline pump anyway.

While looking for a service station, we saw a car with a west German license, which was parked on a side-street. This was certainly a rarity. When we had found a pump, the german car was also there. For once I was glad to see another car, surrounded by a crowd. But at the same time I was sorry for the driver; he had several passengers with him and obviously was no expert at motoring in eastern countries. The endless questions about his car's price in the west, the weight, horse-power and all other imaginable technical details, seemed to confuse him no end, and when he saw me, he came to greet me like a long-lost brother. After shaking my hand and slapping me on the back, as if I had just ridden a racehorse he owned to victory, he explained that he had come from Berlin—West Berlin, he was quick to add—to visit some of his wife's relatives.

The curious crowd now surrounded both of us. The man from West Berlin was still very nervous. He put his hand possessively, or perhaps it was beseachingly on my shoulder, drew one of the service station operators to us with his other hand and stammered:

"Well, you see, both of us have come here as—friends, as—visitors, in order to—to—visit and to . . ."

"How many liters of gasoline do you wish?" the service station attendant asked in flawless German. It was clear that he was not of Polish extraction.

I knew how the man from West Berlin felt. When one comes to these countries for the first time, it is as if one were in another world and one believes that it is necessary to provide all and sundry with unsolicited information about oneself and one's plans.

The novice from Berlin was a grey-haired man who, I judged, was nervous by nature anyway—a bad start for travels in these parts. After he had replied to all questions as best he could and his car was ready, he bade me farewell and wished me success on my trip; I was sure he really meant himself with his wishes and expressed the hope that all would go well with him, a sentiment he echoed fervently. Then, visibly shaken—perhaps by having met me, or by his minutes at the gasoline pump—he drove away.

It was now our turn at the pump and, while the tank was being filled, I learnt that the attendant who had spoken up before was indeed a German and that there were still quite a few of his countrymen in and around Lauenburg. Further west, in Stolp, there were even more, I was told. All of them wanted to emigrate as soon as possible, the attendant said, but it would take a long time before they would be able to leave, because many of them faced the usual problem: they had no relatives in Germany.

In the meantime Jacqueline had been very busy with her diary notes. And now, during a rest a short distance west of Lauenburg, I found the following entry:

Service stations and I sworn enemies. When Charles says: "it will only take five minutes, for sure,—I only have to fetch a little screw," then can be certain it will take at least two hours.
In Poland he does not fetch screws—doubt if such things exist here. Still, service station-stops never seem to end. While am sitting here, writing, waiting, this stop about to shatter all records. Charles standing with grey-haired gentleman, surrounded by big crowd, and I believe he's going to grow roots there any moment.
Next to me, at window, there are also little growths, about to take root: five small, blond, blue-eyed children, wearing minimum of clothing, stand there, staring at me. They look rather nice. Nice, silent, amazed. If these Polish, will eat hat.
"Do you speak German?" I ask.
Children grin pleasantly, step from one foot to other like tethered horses, nudge each other with elbows, grin again, but say nothing.
Am convinced they are German, judging by their looks. Try again to talk to them. Hopeless. Experiment with other way: distribute bar of chocolate among them. Try again to get them to talk. Result: more grinning, embarrassed foot-work, nudging,—further silence. My fourth attempt interrupted by two men who come towards me.
"You won't have much success with them," one of the men tells me in German. "These kids can only speak Polish."
Am crushed. Will have to start eating hat.
"They all have german parents," man goes on, saving hat from reluc-

tant molars. "But they were born at a time when the German language could not be spoken. Around here the controls were so tight, that even at home parents were afraid to speak German. Later the children had to go to Polish schools. And now that they are allowed to speak German again, they haven't really started learning yet."

Man sees that children still busy with chocolate I gave them, says something in Polish. Thereupon one, a girl, steps closer to me, looks at me with fierce concentration.

"Dank' scheen!" she manages to gurgle, pronouncing german words of thanks with unbelieveably thick Polish accent. Then all five children turn, race away.

Man who spoke to me is German. His friend is a Pole, but can also speak German. "Learned it during the war," he explains.

The naivety of these two men is incredible. Both would like to emigrate from here. Pole, echoing German, declares he has had enough of life here. Could I not help them? they ask. Try to explain that I would have little or no success, pleading for them at Polish passport office. This they absolutely fail to believe. Surely it would somehow be possible for me to take them across the border.

"I don't know what has gone wrong," the German says with a sigh. "Everything seems to be cursed. I have a brother in South America and another in Germany. I have often written to both, and never got an answer."

"It could be that your letters never left Poland," I suggest. "I hear this happened quite frequently at one time."

"But I put the right stamps on those letters," the German replies, in a tone implying that I have questioned this sense of correctness.

Pole nods agreement. "Oh yes, everything was done according to the rules, for sure. But perhaps such things will work better now. Gomulka does everything better."

"And there are so many of us here who want to leave," the German goes on. "Even some of the Poles, like my friend here, want to go. Perhaps we could all go together. We will have to write to Warsaw."

Have difficulty trying not to show these two my doubts whether Mr.

Gomulka would be pleased by such a letter. Fortunately do not have to say anything more to them, as Charles approaching. In a way these two men seem no older and certainly no more experienced than the five German children who can't speak German.

THE LAST GERMAN DENTIST

Stolp.—At one time, before we started on this trip, I had made a note: "Stolp,—historical ruins of a castle and well-known church belonging to it." Now I was curious to find out what was left of these architectural monuments, indeed of this entire town which once had 47,000 inhabitants.

It was easy to reach the center of the town: on the left a severely damaged church, on the right another, slightly less scarred. Between the two buildings, nothing, absolutely nothing, apart from rubble, some mounds of stones and a twisted lamp post without a lamp. Not far away, however, there was a Russian war memorial, which was very well kept.

The drive from Lauenburg to this town,—now called Slupsk,—had been anything but pleasant. Again we had passed countless fallow fields, and this virtual desintegration of a civilized region depressed us. In the same depressed condition we then stood in the desert which was the center of Stolp, and what we saw worsened our mood. After a while I suggested that we needed to orientate ourselves a little more, rebuild in our minds the town which once had existed in this desert, to find out the names of the churches, where the castle might be and the like.

Once again I looked about, seeking someone whom I might accost. Not far away I saw a man, whose appearance, in this environment, was surprising: he wore a light-grey suit, which had a far better cut than almost anything we had seen in Poland heretofore. His shirt and tie were clean,—a veritable rarity outside Warsaw. He was perhaps in his mid-fifties, and if our presence astonished him, he certainly knew how to hide his feelings.

"Excuse me, but do you speak German?" I asked.

"Of course!" the man replied casually, "I am a German."

In his manner and way of speech he was quite different from the other Germans we had met until then. Had not the surroundings in which we had met precluded the possibility of forgetting—even for a fleeting moment—where we were, one might have thought that we had come across a German in Germany who was somewhat non-plussed that it was necessary to explain his origin, and that someone had thought it necessary to ask him whether he could speak his native tongue. Once this matter had been cleared up, he turned out to be friendly and ready to explain all we wanted to know about Stolp. We were standing in the former business section of the town, he said, going on to tell us that the church beyond the totally destroyed area was the former "Garnison" church, while the ruins next to it were the remains of the castle. The church nearer to us, had been called St. Mary's.

"You are rather lucky," the man said with a bitter smile, "years ago, you couldn't have seen both our churches at the same time from this location. The entire business section of Stolp would have been in your line of vision."

Introductions were soon over and we learnt that we had met a local dentist, the last German in his profession in this town, perhaps, he thought, the last in the whole of Eastern Pomerania and East Brandenburg. A lively conversation ensued.

Our surroundings were most dicouraging, but the dentist appeared determined to ignore this, preferring to act like a man receiving foreign visitors in his home town under perfectly normal conditions. He asked if we would not like to drop in at his home for a cup of coffee. While this would have been a pleasant break in our routine, we felt that our tight schedule would not permit it; and so we continued our conversation amidst the ruins of Stolp.

The dentist had spent the war years as a dental surgeon in the German navy and had been demobilized in 1945. Having married rather late in life, he had had young children at that time. His wife was a native of Pomerania, and seeking a quiet place in which to settle with his family, he had moved to Stolp.

"We never dreamed that life would become so bad here," he said. And bad it had become. First came the Russians and, as the dentist put it, "smashed whatever they did not set on fire. People were deported, beaten and shot. It was a reign of terror." Then the Russians were replaced by the Poles and although the terror continued, the Polish administration turned out to be a vast improvement. Once the Poles had established themselves firmly, "life ceased being a daily adventure in which one had doubtful chances of survival, and became a battle for existance with an administration and a population who never missed a chance to show their profound hate of Germans and Germany."

During this time the dentist made no effort to leave the territory under Polish administration. In part he believed that the occupation was merely temporary and in part he felt an obligation towards the other Germans who still lived in this area to continue his dental practice. He was never altogether prevented from carrying out his work, for soon he was one of the few dentists in the region; above all, he was the only German dentist, and hence the only one to whom his many countrymen would come for treatment. Apart from the remaining inhabitants of Stolp itself, the number of Germans in this area was swelled by the many who were held as forced labour by the Russians and employed on the large estates of Pomerania which had been confiscated. This forced labour policy was later continued by the Polish administration and some Germans were still on the former estates today.

It had never been easy to provide these people with proper dental care. After the Polish administration had turned communist, our informant had been required to become a state dentist and to work in a clinic. His monthly pay as a fulltime "dental burocrat" was 1,200 Zloty,—or about the same as a semi-skilled worker. Just as the worker, the dentist could not live on this salary, particularly, since he already had four daughters at this time and his wife was expecting a fifth child. To make matters worse, the dentist's health was failing, and he had to request—and was granted—permission to reduce his working hours at the clinic by half.

"You can imagine," he went on to tell us, "that my new salary of 600 Zloty a month would have brought my family to the brink of starvation in a very short time. So out of necessity and also because I wanted to help, I started a private practice again. It soon turned out that this was no way to protect my health. Quite to the contrary. But never mind. During those half-days of practice at home I never saw less than fifteen, sometimes twenty patients! It was like that almost until now. And financially I am also no better off, because these people cannot pay much. But at least I've always had the satisfaction of being able to help my compatriots."

Nor was the domestic life in the dentist's family any too easy. When the oldest daughters reached school-age, they had to go to Polish schools. German schools did not exist, until three years ago. But even then the dentist did not send his children there, because he felt that the teachers, who were all Poles, did not speak German well enough: "the children don't learn anything in those schools," he said. "But my girls have learnt German just the same, because I brought a 'school' into my home: I took a former German teacher into my house as a boarder."

Now the five children speak both languages fluently; the dentists wife also speaks Polish, and in fact, had to become a Polish citizen because she was a native of this area which the administration now officially considers part of Poland.

Not being a native of the region, this rule did not apply to the dentist nor did he learn the language. "And I'll never learn Polish now," he said, "because my time here is almost up. The Germans are leaving this area now,—one family after another. I can tell by my practice. Almost every day I have fewer patients. And so I feel that I have done my duty and that I can go too. I am also thinking of my children. One of these days they have to get proper schooling, not just something improvised. I cannot and will not have them grow up like this, without a real education and without a real country they can call their own. I myself am not so excited by this idea of emigrating. At my age it's not easy to make a complete break and start life all over again. But it has to be."

The dentist told us that he has a brother in West Germany and this will make it possible to move his family there. It seemed admirable that this man, whose close relatives in the west would have made emigration possible a while ago, had stayed here so long.

Even the move which was now being planned was not to be undertaken hurriedly. Some months ago the dentist had been on a visit to Berlin, in order to orientate himself and to overcome what he termed "the isolation of the last twelve years". But the visit had of necessity been short and he had left, still feeling strange. He spoke hesitantly of the West and of "the entirely different mode of life" there.

"But somehow we will manage alright," he said, speaking more to himself than to us. "I have been told that the West is very generous in such cases.'

The signs of uncertainty and isolation became even more apparent, when this educated man who once surely knew the ways of the world added naively:

"I am told that West Germany is the richest country in the world. They are said to drown in money!"

On the other hand he told of western ignorance concerning life in this region. Colleagues whom he had met in Berlin had asked him, how it was that in all the years of intensive work in Stolp he had not managed to save some money and to build himself a new home.

"It is evident that they had no conception of how we live here," he said. "I had to tell them: 'good heavens, what notions you have! Don't you know that after a month of hard, hard work, there is often not enough money in the house on the first of the month in order to pay the food bill for the family?' And then I had to tell my colleagues: 'think of the money I earn, and of the fact that a suit like the one I am wearing costs 3,000 to 4,000 Zloty, and that it costs me 7,000 Zloty just to heat my house!' Yes, I had to tell them all this. They had no idea what it is like to live here. I could have summed it all up for them in one word: hopeless!

Then the dentist concluded: "Really, it is hopeless to live here, and that is why I am leaving, although I really do not want to. I have done what I considered to be my duty, I have hoped that there would be real improvements,—the one thing has been done, the other never came to pass."

While we talked with the dentist, heard about his unusual life and told him something about the West, we had the impression that his calm manner and the matter-of-fact way in which he had met us was a sort of shield, a protection for him. It could well be that he was not nearly as calm as he appeared, for he felt that he was no longer the man of the world he once was or thought himself to have been. After all, his normal life had ended twelve—perhaps even eighteen years ago. But he did not wish to show his doubts and uncertainties, wanting to continue to appear like a man of stature and social position who lived in his home town, peacefully practicing an honourable profession.

Yet the protective reaction was nonetheless noticeable—perhaps just because of the very casualness and calm with which the dentist conducted himself while he told his story; even at the very end of our conversation his outward composure had not been disturbed:

"How about that cup of coffee?" he asked pleasantly, as if we had just met at a busy street corner three hundred miles west of here.

A glance at our watches told us that it was time to move on. We excused ourselves and left the last German dentist in the former German north-east.

"CHOMMINK ROOMS, GRETTEST QUIETUDITY!"

Stolpmünde.—This former Baltic Sea resort is now called Ustka. The short drive from Stolp to this community took us through well-kept fields. We wondered whether these were the state farms or other confiscated estates mentioned by the dentist, on which the German population had been put to work; however, the countryside was well-neigh deserted and we could not find anyone who might give us reliable information. The neat-looking fields led us to hope that Stolpmünde might also be in good condition. But like the trip from Stolp, this hope did not last long. Ustka seems to have become a naval station; the streets are filled with sailors and the whole community looks as military bases do the world over: full of the marks and leavings of young men who know that their stay will be limited and anonymous. The general negligence found everywhere in these territories made this negative impression even more complete.

I doubt if we were ever stared at with more open-mouthed astonishment than here. This may well have been the first time that a foreign car cruised through this base without an official escort; that we were able to do this shows once again how much Poland has changed in recent times. In Hungary, Czechoslovakia, Yugoslavia and in pre-Gomulka Poland such a leasurely drive through a military community of this kind would have been unthinkable or—if attempted—would have had serious consequences. But, in order not to take too much advantage of this liberalization, we did not protract our visit unneccesarily, nor did we take any photographs.

Then we drove along a small country road leading south and returned to the main highway Danzig-Stettin a few miles west of Stolp.

Between the coast and the highway we again found farms in comparatively good condition; the more startling was the state in which we found the land between Stolp and the next town, Schlawe: here fields which had clearly been first-rate farm land, were well on the way towards becoming steppe, while other sections were turning into unkept woodlots. As the wilderness grew apace, the last reminders of cultivation were still to be found: clumps of fruit trees, manure heaps and ploughed furrows thickly overgrown with grass. But beside the grass the only seeds to have taken root here in the last years were those which had drifted over from the trees once planted on the horizon as wind-shelter for the excellent farms. Now these seeds were allowed to destroy much of the land their progenitors had protected.

Schlawe.—This little town half-way between Stolp and Köslin is now called Slawno. The attractive city-gate at the eastern entrance to the town is well preserved, while the western gate is severely damaged. Most of the core of the town between these two gates is ruined. The Parish church stands alone in the center of a large field of rubble, the upper half of its steeple missing, its inside totally burnt out. On the fringe of this wrecked town center, quite a few houses are still standing, although many of these are also damaged. Once the population of Schlawe was 9,000. It is doubtful whether more than a mere fraction of this number of new inhabitants has been settled here to date.

Köslin.—This town is now the capital of a wojewodztwo, a province, and has become more important than it was in German times. In Warsaw we were told that the city has more inhabitants than previously. Its new name in Koszalin.

As soon as we arrived, we noticed that the war must have wrought havoc here, but also, that an effort was being made to rebuild. There were still large gaps in the rows of houses, but particularly in the middle of town, much new construction was to be seen. A rather broad shopping street was lined on both sides by post-war buildings. They were two storeys high, monnotonous in design and smaller than others presently under construction; the latter looked as if they were destined to become large office buildings or apartment blocks. The majority of the low structures had bare brick outer walls, which gave them an unfinished look, and they seemed to have been built hurriedly. This street reminded us of a certain mining towns in Canada or the United States, which grow up like mushrooms around iron, gold or uranium mines.

It was evening. An unusually large crowd filled both sidewalks and parts of the street itself. There was no vehicular traffic and the people stopped and stared in disbelief as we drove slowly by. We felt as if we were in a cage, being exhibited to an amazed public. It was not a pleasant experience.

143

In Zoppot we had been told that the Hotel "Miejski" in Köslin, though not an "Orbis" hotel, was nonetheless "quite good", and that we could safely reserve a room there. Now we had to find this hotel. We stopped five or six times and asked for directions, but no one ever heard of a place by that name. Then two men who spoke fluent German explained to me, that the Hotel "Miejski" was really the Hotel "Europa" and was to be found in the next street. We followed their directions and were soon convinced that the men had made a mistake. A sign, reading "Europa" was attached to a tiny and indescribably dirty house, which might perhaps have been a tavern, although even this was difficult to imagine: all the windows on the ground floor were smashed; on the upper storey there were a few unbroken windows but they were unspeakably dirty and had no curtains; there seemed to be no entrance to the building, nor was there any sign of life around it.

We were about to drive off when the two men came running towards us and assured us again that this was the Hotel "Miejski". We looked at each other; it just couldn't be right! But if it was, well—good night, or rather, bad night!

We continued to cruise through the town, but failed to find anyone who could give us further information about our hotel.

At last we pulled up at the railway station. Two militiamen stood there surrounded by a group of idlers. They all came to us as soon as we had halted, but could not solve our problem. There was a good deal of debate in Polish and finally one of the militiamen let us know that his comrade would drive with us to show the way. Did he really know where we were to go? I asked. Absolutely, the policeman seemed to tell us. His comrade was so embarrassed he had to be pushed into our car, which was done to the accompaniment of much jeering and whistling on the part of the idlers.

In no time we had reached the street where the so-called Hotel "Miejski" or "Europa" was located. We began to feel grim. But the policeman said: "go on, go on—first right, then left!" and we passed the establishment.

"You see!" I said to Jacqueline triumphantly, "I knew,—it coudn't be that bad."

But our feelings of relief did not last long. Suddenly the policeman called out: "halt!" I looked around. Everywhere militiamen! Scores of them, a whole regiment of them, along with their jeeps and squad cars and "Black Marias"! We had been taken to police-headquarters. Before we could ask what was going to happen, our guide had leaped from the car and run towards a group of his colleages. There a lively discussion ensued.

"A night in the cooler might be the solution," Jacqueline mumbled. But it never came to that. Our man returned and reentered the car. Four of his companions followed and, leaning through the windows, gave us long and complicated directions of which we failed to understand anything but the ever-recurring words, "Hotel Miejski". Our guide nodded wisely. Now, fully armed with information, we could really start on our way.

Again we drove through many streets of Köslin, and soon—oh horror, could it be true?—we were back in the same familiar street of "Miejski-Europa" fame! Our policeman was undisturbed by the fact that the establishment seemed to have no entrance. He told me to drive around the next corner, then bade me stop before a little courtyard, separated from the street by a wooden fence with a gate in it. The yard, its contents and the surroundings shacks resembled a small and decidedly neglected farm. I saw some tumble-down outbuildings, with ladders leading to haylofts, two broken farm carts, a pile of firewood, several garbage containers filled to overflowing and a number of chicken and pigs. The gate into the yard was too narrow for our car and I nearly knocked the entire fence over while trying to drive in. This, to all intents and purposes precluded an overnight stay in the hotel or whatever it was, as it would be quite impossible to leave the car in the street. When I asked the policeman about a garage elsewhere, he looked surprised and shook his head.

But something had to be done and so we decided at least to have a look at the place and to leave the car in the street the while. During this short time a crowd of more than a hundred people had gathered around us. I thought they looked particularly wild, and moreover, the customary investigational rocking of the car had already begun. Quickly we determined to follow our usual routine: I was to stay behind while Jacqueline went on inspection; I gave the militiaman a handful of cigarettes and asked him to accompany her. He seemed delighted and the two of them departed. Then I mounted guard and prepared to recite my litany: price, horse-power, cylinder bore, consumption of gasoline, pressure in the tires, price, horse-power, cylinder bore . . . .

And now I had better let Jacqueline record her adventures in the Hotel "Miejski" or "Europa" in her own words:

Could laugh or cry. Don't know which would be better. Laughing probably preferable, as is good for digestion, and digest I must. Also better not to over-strain tear ducts. Have following to digest:
First we cross courtyard. Militiaman marches beside me. Meet three soldiers accompanied by three girls in red dresses. Yes, indeed, red dresses. Do not fail to recognize this warning light made of cloth, (should say, "red warning light"). But duty is duty and besides would feel no happier guarding car while Charles on this inspection tour. Reach splendid hotel entrance: little door like that of stable. Inside, stable smell, also similar decor. One thing missing: cattle. No human being anywhere. But militiaman knows his way: climbs stairs resembling entrance to chicken-coop, waves me up. Am led to glass door featuring broken glass. Militiaman points inside, says:
"In there management."
Go inside. On camp bed lounges barrel-type female of the species, wearing not too much clothing but lots of fake jewelry. Has cigarette in corner of mouth and is engaged in discourse with young man who stands before her.
"Ah ha!" declares management in managerial tone and inspects me from head to foot.
"Wassermann", I reply in best don't-understand-anything tone of voice.

146

"*We telephoned from Zoppot to reserve a room.*"

"*Yayes, yayes,*" *says management, without stirring from camp bed, and continues in language of indeterminate origin: "chommink rooms, grettest quietudity!*"

At this moment, as if to illustrate "grettest quietudity", piercing scream is heard and half-dressed girl gallops down corridor. Half-dressed soldier follows, roaring with laughter.

"*There haff you, room zwelve,*" *says management giving me a key, while still reclining on camp bed. Key comes from bunch dangling at her barrel waist.*

Have actually had enough, but long years of marriage to reporter foster reporter-curiosity. Take key, wave to trusty militiaman and wander off in search of room twelve.

Corridor affords splendid view into chommink rooms with grettest quietudity. Several doors are opened revealing girls with red or no dresses and contiguous male co-tenants. Militiaman also very interested observer.

Reach room twelve, unlock same, conscript militiaman to employ broad police-shoulder for purpose of forcing door open. Furniture very chommink: two camp beds with matresses, but no linen, no blankets. One table with wash-basin and water jug. Full stop. Nothing more.

Turn around, walk past two soldiers who whistle at me, return key to management.

"*Wot is?*" *asks management.*

"*Everything's fine,*" *I say, "but first we have to go and eat. We'll come back later.*"

"*Is good, come wann you will,*" *says management. Notice that she winks at militiaman.*

Have sudden idea: management thinks he is militiaman Wassermann. Never mind. Don't mind anything anymore. Return to car, fight my way through to real militiaman Wassermann, who is on hardship post surrounded by vast crowd.

Charles recognizes situation by one look at my face, starts the motor

and makes furious noises with car horn. My policeman climbs in
with me.
"Is this the only hotel in Koszalin?" I ask.
"Only one," he says. "Nice, eh?"
"Chommink" I mutter to myself. Then ask the policeman if there is
also a restaurant in this town.
"That too,' he replies proudly. "I show".
Ask myself where we'll sleep. Perhaps it's better not to ask such silly
questions. Compared to Hotel "Miejski"-"Europa" our car is "chom-
mink room", with "grettest quietudity"!

Jacqueline looked pale as she returned to the car. We drove according
to the policeman's directions through several small side streets. We
now noticed many drunks everywhere; one lay between the sidewalk
and a half shattered house. No one seemed to take any notice of him;
even our policeman only shrugged his shoulders when he saw the man.
Soon we were back in the busy shopping street trough which we had
passed on first entering Köslin. Unfortunately the only restaurant in
town turned out to be on this street, which meant leaving our car
literally "in the hands" of a truly overwhelming multitude. But we
know that one warm meal per day is important during a strenuous
journey such as this, and we decided to take a chance. For a moment
I wondered whether the policeman might serve as guard but noticed
that he was looking at his watch and beginning to become restless.
He was probably off duty by now and eager to get home. We thanked
him for his help, gave him some more cigarettes and he went on
his way.
We are now sitting in the "Baltyk" restaurant, which can only be
described as a tame offspring of the Hotel "Miejski". Jacqueline has
already recognized a number of people whom she had previously seen
during her inspecting tour. Incidently, I have just discovered with the
help of our Polish dictionary that Hotel "Miejski" simply means
"municipal hotel". The people in Zoppot evidently had no conception

of local conditions and did not even know what the real name of the hotel in this town was.

The restaurant is unbelievably full. A twisting mass of humanity, reminiscent of Allenstein, leaps around an infinitessimal dance floor. An orchestra of six musicians produces an insane cacophony of sounds which is supposed to be jazz.

At first we were told that there was not a table to be had. But it is remarkable how friendly people are: amidst a group of others who also wanted tables, we stood wondering how we were going to get this day's warm meal, when somebody went to talk to the musicians who declared themselves willing to give us the table at which they usually sit during intermission. We were very grateful, although the table is located immediately below the plattform on which the six men make their frightful noise.

We have learned a good many new polish words, among them "barszcz", the red-beet soup, which is practically a national dish; "sznycel wiedenski" veal cuttlet à la viennoise; "piwo", beer; in this way we were able to order a meal.

We have now eaten and completed our diary entries and are waiting for the breakfast supplies we have ordered. Since it looks as though we are going to have to sleep in the car this night, we decided to get all our supplies right now, including hot water for the morning's coffee and the mid-day soup. It's better to be prepared.

We had some trouble trying to explain to the waitress that we wanted to have our two big thermos bottles cleaned and filled with hot water and that we also needed four hard boiled eggs, bread and butter. I was just looking up the necessary words in our dictionary, when an ancient waiter in a dirty white jacket came to our table.

"Wos hetten S' denn gern?"—"What would you like to have?" he asked in the broadest viennese dialect of German.

Despite my amazement I explained our wishes and the waiter replied: "Don't you worry, we'll have that for you in a jiffy!" and he translated what I had said into Polish, whereupon the waitress departed with our thermos bottles. Then the waiter turned to me and smiled:

"Don't be surprised that I speak German," he said, still speaking idiomatic Viennese. "I'm an old imperial soldier. Went through the whole war with the Kaiser's artillery. Those were times I tell you. But now! my God, if my sergeant had seen this place here, he'd have said to me, 'Josef', he'd have said to me, 'Josef, this here place is a pig sty!' Now you'd better excuse me. Ive got to go back to work.' With that Josef disappeared. But, believe it or not, here come our supplies! On into battle and into the dark night!

GHOSTS AND BAND MUSIC

On the road to Kolberg.—That our car was unharmed while we were in the "Baltyk" restaurant in Köslin, is partly due to the fact that, without knowing it, we had a volunteer guard in attendance.

When we left the restaurant the street was completely blocked by countless curious people. Other vehicles—had there been any besides our own,—would have been unable to pass.

Despite the closely packed crowd, nobody touched our car and we soon saw why: a small man with a thin mustache and a tired face marched continuously around it, shoving anyone who came too close back into the multitude without the least ceremony. As we appeared, the guard approached me with a smile and shook my hand.

"How d'you do?" he said, speaking English without a trace of an accent. "How's things back in Canada?"

I said that everything seemed to be alright, and the man replied that he was glad to hear it, because he hadn't heard anything for a while from back there. It turned out that he had spent twelve years working at the Ford Motor Company of Canada plant in Windsor, Ont. And our car not only had a Canadian license it was also a Ford!

"Looked after her a bit for you," he said very seriously. "Must say, they've sorta changed the model since I was over there last."

"When was that?" I asked.

"1946", he replied.

"And then you went back to Poland?"

"That's right. I wanted to go home."

"But 'home' wasn't Koszalin?"

"God forbid!" he exclaimed. "I come from Warsaw, but I didn't like it there after a few years. So when they said that there were good chances for a better life in the new territory, I came here. I'll tell you I shoulda stayed in Canada. But sometimes your feelings are stronger 'n your brains.—Aw, well, at least I could look after the old Ford for you. So long, see ya in Canada!"

He again shook my hand and I had the feeling that he was deeply moved. I wanted to say a few friendly words to him but he had already vanished in the crowd.

We managed to slip into the car and to drive on without injuring anybody. A few minutes later we left the main highway to Stettin and continued in a north-westerly direction towards Kolberg.

Just now we have stopped about half way along the 28 mile drive from Köslin to Kolberg, made these last diary entries and debated: should we park somewhere away from this highway and sleep in the car or should we go on? We could prepare two reasonably comfortable sleeping quarters on the front and rear seats; on the other hand, it's a clear moon-lit night and after a cup of coffee we would certainly be able to go on as far as Kolberg. There is also nothing important on our programme between here and Kolberg, so it would not matter if we drove at night. In this way we would save time and make to-morrow's trip to Stettin shorter. But where should we sleep then? Probably in the car after all. Judging by our experiences in Köslin, it's almost certain that Kolberg will be even worse.

While we think these things over, Jacqueline has already brought out the thermos bottle. We are making coffee. We'll go on.

Kolberg (Kolobrzeg).—The tape recorder is turned on. I am holding the microphone in my hand and driving slowly through the city. Through the "city"! A cruel joke. Ghosts stand on guard here, ghosts of the dead, never truly burried Baltic Sea spa, Kolberg. Like the fleshless fingers of a skeleton hand the chimneys and smoke stacks reach into the mild moon-lit night, feeling, searching desperately for that which once belonged to them, their flesh and blood,—the houses, the hotels, all the things which once have stood here.

And then the walls! half-shattered, half-crumbled they stand here like profiles of ghostly faces, with yellow eyes, where once the windows were, with gaping mouths, horribly tisted as in the last moments of extreme pain when life was taken from them.

Bones lie about, this way and that: they are the beams and pillars—wood and steel,—between which there once were rooms,—rooms offering security and warmth and domestic life. Now, they are nothing but naked, bare bones, shattered in part, senseless, purposeless, lifeless. And at all this,—that is the irony of it,—nature smiles! Smiles and grows and blooms! The trees in the streets between the ghostly ruins are fresh-green and laden with beautiful leaves and blossoms. The grass next to the sidewalks whereon hardly a man treads but many a shadow, this grass is thick and little flowers grow in it as if many-coloured marbles had been strewn about here by a playing child. And near-by, like a never ending pulse, the sea rolls across the beach and trickles away again, in response to another breath by a gigantic organism. Organism.—Life.

Life and death meet here and one shudders and wishes that this moon-drenched night would end.

For half an hour we have driven aimlessly through this town. Like rigid, unblinking eyes our headlight beams have bored into the darkness under the trees. We have seen no human beings.

Now, we can hear something! Click, clack, click, clack—footsteps—the footsteps of several men with hobnails or steel heels on their boots. Click, clack, click, clack.—They're coming closer. Our motor is very quiet, we can hear the steps clearly. There! Now they are caught in the beam of our light. Six militiamen. They stop. They stare into the bright light. One of them waves his hand. I turn the head lights off, the parking lights on. They are coming towards us.

Five of them are walking around the car, one comes to my window. I must turn the tape recorder off.

They've gone. The recorder is on again.

"Hotel? Hotel?" I had said to the policeman at my window.

He had nodded, pointed into the darkness, into the ruins. He had spoken a few sentences and pointed again. Now we are driving once more.

A hotel is nowhere in sight. Only more ruins, more ghosts.

"There! look, there it is!"

That was Jacqueline. She always sees these things first. To our right there's really an undamaged house, alone among the wreckage. Over its entrance a small but electrically illuminated sign: "Hotel".

Jacqueline is going in; I am to guard the car. Against whom? Against what? Probably against an onslaught of ghosts.

The tape recorder has been turned off long ago; now it's standing, together with the other technical equipment and the suitcases called the "short stay group", in a primitive but at least not too dirty room. A woman is in charge of this small hotel. She regarded us with suspicion because we arrived so late. She does not speak any foreign language and Jacqueline had difficulties persuading her to rent us a room. First, 38 Zloty had to be put on the table, the complicated registration form completed and our passports handed over, before the woman would show one of her rooms. But Jacqueline assures me that this is a vast improvement over room number twelve in Köslin. Certainly there are no soldiers here and no girls in red dresses.

But there can be no thought of sleep yet. The drive through Kolberg was an upsetting experience. Moreover, somewhere outside, a street-corner loudspeaker—the kind found in all communist countries—has been turned on full blast. In the middle of the night military band music echos through the ghostly streets. We are sitting under the only source of light in our room,—a naked bulb hanging from the ceiling, —bringing our diaries up to date, studying road maps and hoping that fatigue will soon close our eyes. However, this may still take some time, because apart from the noise we are also being plagued by an unpleasant rash; it is probably due to the food at the "Baltyk".

I have been looking out of the window for a while. Facing me, across the street, to my left and my right I saw the ghostly ruins once more —grey and frightening in the gentle moonlight. Before them the beautiful trees. Behind, between, above them, the rhytmic military music of Poland. I thought: here are the symbols of this unfortunate territory: the ruins of the past, the untroubled splendour of nature, and all this permeated by the rhythmic, mechanical, steel-cold sound of military band music,—the voice of the all-powerful state.

A strong drink of whisky. To bed, to bed!

Early morning.—Kolberg looks hardly more beautiful or cheerful in the sparkling sunlight of early morning. On another drive through the city we did see a few people—mostly soldiers—but the ruins still dominate every scene; many of them look as if they had been gradually withered by a form of atrophy. Countless buildings, particularly those near the sea, are destroyed in an unusual way: they have neither vanished, as has so often been the case where we have passed, nor have they been reduced to shapeless heaps of rubble; in Kolberg they are perfectly preserved skeletons, while everything which gave this framework form and character has gone. We drove through that part of the city where the resort hotels must have stood and found one skeleton after another. We stopped near the beach, before a frightening ruin which was probably the well-known hotel "Strandschloss". I swam in the sea. The water was cold and refreshing but the deserted beach and the wilderness which was once a well kept park depressed us greatly.

Driving back through the former town,—one can only refer to it as such,—we also saw the heavily damaged St. Mary's Church. This community once had 38,000 inhabitants. Today a few thousands may be here, although we had the impression that it could be no more than a few hundreds.

We experienced a feeling of relief when we left Kolberg.

Treptow.—This small town with the former ducal castle is now called Trzebiatow. One can still imagine that this was a pleasant little provincial town with some attractive architecture and a quiet life of its own. But one has to rely solely on the gift of imagination, for there are no other aids to recall the past. As we drove through ill-kept cobble-stone streets, we searched for a word which would describe the present Treptow aptly. Then it occured to both of us: a dunghill. I do not like to use such terms when referring to communities where people live, but here no other word would do. No war-time damage is to be seen in this town and yet it looks almost as neglected as those which have suffered greatly in the fighting and bombing. Dirt and garbage are everywhere, walls crumble, windows are broken and covered over with paper. Poverty is to be seen wherever one looks,— poverty and soldiers. Of all the undestroyed cities we have visited until now, Treptow is the dirtiest and poorest.

In this area we again saw much steppe-like fallow land. It would seem that in this region, in which broken wind-mills stand like memorials to another time, no more than a quarter of the available farm land in in use. It's also astonishing that market-gardening is so rare. We have seen no fields of carrots and even potatoes are less frequently planted than one would expect. Beets are a crop seen occasionally, while peas, beans and the like seem not to have been planted at all in this part of the former german territories.

In Schwirsen, now called Swierzno, a little village as poor as the others, we saw a typical example of the present inhabitants' indifference: a farm house had been severely damaged by bombs,—that is to say, part of it had been completely laid low; it stood exactly as it had been hit, and it was possible to look into the former rooms, where walls were missing on three sides. Yet people were living in another wing of the house, which was damaged but not destroyed. Evidently they were quite unconcerned by what was happening to the part of the building they did not require for their daily life. Pride of ownership is unknown here; and no wonder.

Cammin in Pomerania.—A town of 6,000 inhabitants has become a hamlet. As so often, the center of what is now Kamien Pomorski, is a field of ruins which has barely been cleaned up. Around the center there are some ill-kept houses.

The lack of interest among the population is so great here, that even German signs on houses and former factories have not been painted over. We saw a clearly legible shield reading: "A. Krüger, Tailor" on a house in which there has not been a shop for more than a decade, and the words: "Export Brewery, Bros. Voerkelius" on the remains of what was evidently a large concern.

As in most of these cities it was impossible to buy supplies, except for bread, poor-quality cheese and unpleasantly maladourous sausages. From this one can gather how little food the citizens can buy unless they have special connections,—perhaps to a private farmer. But sweets, ice cream and beer are always to be had, being sold in wooden huts which stand by the dozen in every small town; they look as if nailed together in a hurry, a stop-gap, like almost everything else in the daily life of the people in these regions.

Leaving Cammin, we drove in a northerly direction to the Baltic Sea coast, and a village once called *Bad Berg-Dievenow,* now renamed Dziwnow. The village is located on a thin strip of land which separates the "Camminer Bodden",—a bay on which Cammin is located,—from the Baltic Sea. Once this was a popular holiday resort; today little evidence of such a past can be found, save for a few shabby hotels and villas. Instead of holiday guests the place is filled with soldiers. We have stopped here for a brief rest and are now about to continue to Wollin, Swinemünde and then to Stettin.

On the road to Stettin.—On the island of Wollin the farms look somewhat better then in the district around Cammin and Kolberg. But here too woodlots have begun to exceed their former bounderies and some earstwhile fields have become unintended tree nurseries.

The community *Wollin* (Wolin) which is listed on our polish map in large letters, turned out to be a little group of houses and a factory of which we could not say whether it was in use or not. We did not see much of Swinemünde. Now colled Swinoujscie, the place is located on the left bank of the river Swine, immediately on the border with the DDR. From the opposite shore one can only cross by ferry and since this would have entailed passing two polish war-ships which were anchored in the river, and mingling with the many soldiers hereabouts, we decided that photography would be unwise and a trip to the city a waste of time.

Now, while driving through the magnificent forest near Stettin we have stopped once more and eaten a belated lunch. During this time came what we had feared since the beginning of this journey: the possibility of a irreparable breakdown of our car.

I was putting oil into the motor, and in an absent-minded moment placed the half-filled can of oil on the car's battery. The can touched both poles of the battery, and it happened: a dreadful bang, a white flame and a little cloud of smoke. Jacqueline tells me that at this moment my face was just as green as the colour of our car. Certain that I had short-circuited the electrical system and that we would have to remain forever in the woods north of Stettin I half-walked, half-dragged myself to the driver's seat and, just to prove to myself what an idiot I was, turned the ignition key. The motor started at once! The only damage: the plastic caps which close the battery cells have been shattered. My nerves too.

Jacqueline is currently performing one of her miracles: she's sticking the bits of battery cap together with nail polish,—and succeeding rather well.

In half an hour we should reach Stettin.

FROM THE NEUTRAL TO THE NOTHING AND BACK

Stettin.—I have been standing here, at one and the same spot for almost an hour and I still cannot believe what lies before me! I should be case-hardened by now, should have learned long ago to accept what is inalterable. But I am still horrified.

I am at the "Berliner Tor", a small triumphal arch I had no difficulty recognizing by its elaborate stonemasonry which is currently being repaired. I am looking in a south-easterly direction: to my right there is a large church with a shattered nave and half a roof. Further to the left, on the horizon of my field of vision, there is an even larger building, which might be desribed as a castle.

Between me and the church, between the church and the castle and between the castle and me not a single building is left—not even a ruin. Yet I know that this large triangle was once the center of Stettin, which, after Königsberg was the largest city of the German north-east. Looking at my pre-war Baedecker, I see that this triangle contained streets and squares like the Lindenstrasse and the Paradeplatz, the Grosse Wollweberstrasse and the Mönchenstrasse, the Rossmarkt and Stettin's main shopping street: the Breite Strasse. And between these main thoroughfares there was a spider's web of side-streets and alleys which criss-crossed the area. All this has vanished. Were it not for the still distinguishable three landmarks at the ends of the triangle, and my old documents and photographs, it would be impossible to tell the difference between this and any other vacant space.

One also has to be wary of asking any new citizen of Stettin—or rather Szczecin—to help identify the remaining landmarks; it seems they know little or nothing about the history of the city in which they live. A while ago a man assured me that the church to my right is called the St. Paula Church; the name sounded wrong to me. I took out some old photographs, examined them with a magnifying glass and compared architectural details on the pictures with those of the severely damaged church; soon it was clear, that I was looking at the remains of the famous Jacobi Church. The man I had asked for information watched me during my on-the-spot research and after I had finished, said again that this church had never been called anything but St. Paula's.

Stettin has become totally neutral, a town without a face. It was never one of those "architectural showcase cities", but what notable buildings there were in the "Altstadt"—the oldest part—have either disappeared or have been neutralized by a planned alteration of names and by neglect. The change of population served to complete this neutralization, for all ties with the past were effectively severed. This even makes possible the rebuilding of one or the other monument,— for instance the Berliner Tor; it is no longer called by that name, has no further significance as an historic landmark; to the present citizens of Szczecin it is simply a baroque arch on which some decorations are being mounted.

Due to these developments, Stettin-1957 makes one main impression: that of being a grey provincial town. Not only the destruction contributes to this impression, but almost everything one sees and hears. This is no Danzig, with its classical reconstruction, a cause for discussion, if nothing else; nor is this an Allenstein, a town which—probably in order to please the Masurians—has still maintained its basic character; no, this is just A Place—a place in which many people are required to live in close proximity. This makes the city uninteresting, even repulsive. Since our arrival we have visited many parts of Stettin and beyond our purely negative impressions here in the center, have had no experiences with sufficient impact to make us say: 'if later we want to remind ourselves of Stettin, then we are going to think of this or that event, this or that picture!'

Besides the Jacobi Church, other important landmarks have not fared much better: the castle can barely be recognized. The so-called "New City Hall" is an empty shell. The Königstor, or King's Gate, is pockmarked by direct hits. St. John's Church (Johannes Kirche) is destroyed.

The right bank of the river Oder is a shambles of unrecognizable ruins. Arriving from the east, one first reaches this part of town and in order to get to the center, must drive through a labyrinth of temporary roads and pontoon-bridges. Then, moving up from the river towards the city one passes dreadful street corners, where burnt-out shells of houses stand exactly as they stood in 1945. In these ugly carcasses, rats have found a paradise and half-wild cats ideal hunting grounds; here and there hungry-looking dogs, which seem to have no master and no shelter, howl and bak. As in surrealistic drawings, crooked and broken street lamps lean at crazy angles on the corners. The most modern theater set would seem conservatively realistic compared to these scenes.

On the other hand, many streets of Stettin were not damaged during the war. Particularly in an area around the former Kaiser-Wilhelm-Platz. But residential and shopping distrits of this kind usually have no individual characteristics; should there have been any in Stettin, they have long been erased by neglect and the indifference of the people who live here.

Yet there are moments when one feels that Stettin is a metropolis. There are more shops than in most Polish cities with the exception of Warsaw, there is more traffic and one notices more reasonably well-dressed people. But even in this truncated rest of a big town there is no feeling of individuality; again merely a conglomeration of human beings who, by their presence create a certain variety. The greater volume of traffic makes contact with the people more difficult for us; we cannot park so easily, they cannot lounge as much, everyone is pushed on. There is no shortage of drunks here either. A little while ago we watched as three militiamen in a jeep drove up before our hotel, the "Orbis-Continental", went in and dragged a totally inebriated man out of this supposedly best establishment in town.

Quite a lot of new construction is going on in the neutral-grey apartment- and shopping- area. Large blocks of flats are in different stages of completion. The tenants move in long before the buildings are finished, proof—if such is needed—that the housing shortage is as grave here as elsewhere. Under these circumstances one wonders why the large villas and town houses north of the former Bismark and Kaiser Wilhelm squares are not being used as living quarters but as club houses for Party functionaries and army officers.

One positive fact is to be recorded here: although our hotel looks dirty from the outside and the public rooms have a certain "Orbis" odour, our bedroom is quite pleasant. We have high hopes of being able to rest a little.

Pyritz.—This morning at breakfast in Stettin we met a western diplomat from Warsaw, whom we have known for a while. He was also travelling through these territories for the first time; the previous day he had been in Pyritz, a nearby town now called Pyrzyce; he shook his head when he heard that we also planned to go there. "That should be quite an experience for you," he said.

It was an experience.—Our visit to Pyritz began with a police control. This time none of our documents interested the militiaman who stopped us; instead I was subjected to a long lecture, of which I did not understand a single word. But it was not hard to guess what it was all about: the policeman had a helper—a thin, small, terribly excited little man—who came rushing up, clutching a stop-watch, and provided the militiaman with a few breathless morsels of information. It seemed we had broken the speed law. I went into my tried-and-true ostrich or don't-understand-a-word act. Thereupon the policeman took out a large and very dirty notebook into which he wrote my name and a few other details. I expected that I would have to pay a fine of a few Zloty. But no. The policeman saluted and the matter was settled.

Then we entered Pyritz. First we saw some blocks of flats which were probably built in pre-war times, followed by others, which had evidently been completed recently. Before the war Pyritz was famous for its medieval city wall which surrounded the entire town and was considered the best-preserved monument of its kind in Pomerania.

"Was" is the right expression. The entire old city inside the walls has vanished, save for the ruin of a church, a few shattered houses and a shed-like building which may have been something like a plumber's workshop. Nothing else—absolutely nothing. Of the city wall itself only a part of the northern and eastern side remains. These wall-sections contain severely damaged parts of two watch towers and small pieces of several "Wiekhäuser", houses built into the walls and surmounted by steeples which were used for the defence of the town.

All but one of the well-known city-gates are gone and even this one is barely recognizeable as such. A street, famous for its fine medieval buildings, which led to the North Gate has disappeared along with the gate, and it took me an hour to find what is left: a foot-path, which twists its way through thick bushes and rubble. I then took some pictures there to remind us of this desolate place.

For a while I continued to wander through the heap of rubble which was once the town of Pyritz. The people whom I met looked like gypsies. Some of them rode on primitive carts, drawn by ancient nags. The shabbiness and extreme poverty of the new citizens of Pyritz added to the gloom of this cemetary of a town.

As we drove on in a westerly direction, we noted to our surprise, that workers were rebuilding the tower which once was part of the western gate.

Why as a single tower being rebuilt? Was this the beginning of a large-scale project, or the hobby-horse of an official in a government office? If Pyritz is to be rebuilt in its old form, like Danzig, then it will take at least fifteen years, until this nothing becomes a town once again. If an official is merely trying to build himself an "ivory tower", than he could hardly have chosen a place with a more depressing view in every direction.

The western diplomat had been right: we had indeed had quite an experience.

Lippehne (Lipiany).—Once more fate has played its inscrutable game: Lippehne is hardly twelve miles away from Pyritz; yet these twelve miles have saved this little town on a peninsula in the Wendel lake. Hardly a house has been destroyed here, although most buildings are as neglected as elsewhere. Two splendid archways in late-gothic style at the north and south entrances to the town are well-preserved.

Soldin.—This small town also had two gates once upon a time. Today we could only find one; on it we noticed large Russian lettering, written in whitewash, which we think denote the initials of the Communist Party of Poland; that would seem to be quite apt, for this community, re-baptized Mysliborz, looks rather like an east-Polish or even Russian town. There are few scars of war to be seen here, but the more signs of neglect, and one feels the sleepy atmosphere of a place in which no one wants to be bothered by too many problems. A few people stand in the streets, others sit in front of their houses, often looking quite drunk, although it is mid-morning. The few shops have windows well-protected by sturdy iron bars, but one wonders why: there are hardly any goods on view. A sleepy-looking militiaman stands in the shade of a house and stares into space.

A horse-drawn cart with a bent rear axle is the only vehicle in sight. At the headquarters of the Communist Party a loudspeaker blares march music into the dusty, deserted street.

Neudamm (Debno).—Between Soldin and this town almost all the fields were fallow. It may be that they once belonged to the former estate, which we have just passed. It must have been a fine property. The garden-wall around the imposing villa is still intact and the gate-house is undamaged. The main building looks as if it had been ransacked and smashed deliberately. It is still standing, but it would hardly be worth while to repair it.

For a time we stopped before the entrance, thinking of the immense economic damage caused by such uncontrolled post-war "revange actions" and vandalism. Even though the former owners were driven out, the properties themselves could have been most valuable to near-bankrupt Poland. But instead, many of the estates are still unoccupied today, even if they are not in ruins, thus contributing to rather than alleviating the bancruptcy.

Little Neudamm itself has suffered minor damage, although the usual is to be noted: the center of the town has practically disappeared.

Küstrin.—It is fortunate that we did not arrive here at night, for this town, now called Kostrzyn, would have made as terrifying an impression as Kolberg; just as terrifying and yet different, for while Kolberg is a place of skeleton-houses and ghostly ruins, Küstrin does not even have these: this town at the confluence of the rivers Oder and Warthe, which once had a population of 22,000, to all intents and purposes does not exist any more. A few factories seem to be in operation. Then there are some barracks; these may be for the workers in the factories, or for the ubiquitous soldiers, who are probably on frontier duty, when they are not standing in groups along the main highway. This is a border region. On the other shore of the Oder begins the DDR.

Here and there, between the thick clumps of bushes which have grown up on either side of the road, one can see parts of a wall or the remains of a cellar. In this nothingness, even these pityful mementos are welcome: they are proof that at least at some other time life flourished here.

We stand and stare. Once in a while people in civilian clothes pass us or ancient farm carts rattle over the rough road. We have the impression that the people hereabouts hardly know where they come from, whither they should go.

How should they know? Nothing leads to nothing.

Frankfurt-an-der-Oder.—That part of Frankfurt, which now belongs to Poland, and which lies on the right bank of the river Oder, is called Slubice.

We made most of the trip to this town twice. Many people will probably think the reason childish and it may be that only those will understand our motivation, who are accustomed to traveling in deeply depressing regions such as these. Here one tends to develop an exaggerated attachment to those few personal belongings one carries and which make life a little less drab, a little reminiscent of normal times and conditions. One such object is—or unfortunately I should say was—a leather cigarette-case which Jacqueline once gave me for my birthday. When we stopped for lunch at a clearing in the woods somewhere north of Küstrin, we spread our road maps on the hood of the car, discussed our route, drank coffee and smoked. Then we packed up our "kitchen", folded the map and drove on. The car is green, the cigarette-case was green; it was not sufficiently noticeable on the hood and must have slid to the ground as soon as the car moved.

We drove on, heading for Frankfurt, following the course of the Oder and noticing the wooden watch-towers of the Polish frontier guards. It was quite a while before we wanted to smoke again. And then we noticed the loss. We were both upset, ready to do everything to find this little part of our normal private life. It was a long way back to our picnic spot, and when we reached it, there was no sign of the cigarette case anywhere. Between communities, there is hardly a soul on the highways, but one need only wish fervently that nobody be near a lonely spot in the forest, and someone is sure to pass. Perhaps a man on a bicycle or a farm waggon will be overwhelmed by his find, above all by the twenty cigarettes which were in it.

Polish Frankfurt, which we have now reached belatedly, is a little provincial town, nothing more. In consists of a few streets lined by blocks of flats dating from the years between the wars, the kind built in suburbs everywhere, for these streets were on the outskirts of the real Frankfurt across the river.

We have parked on the banks of the Oder and are looking across to the city in the German Democratic Republic. Two Polish militiamen just passed by and told me that this was a place for "nix fotografieren"— no photography.

We are near a new-looking bridge across the frontier-river; the border control points of Poland and the DDR are located at each end of the span. Neither a vehicle nor a pedestrian has crossed the bridge during the half hour we have been here. The militiaman who came by again, and turned out to be very friendly, told us that only during the International Trade Fair at Poznan was there any volume of travel at this —or for that matter any other—border station between Poland and the DDR.

Before driving to this vantage point by the river, we pulled up at a near-by filling station; the woman attendant and I got to talking and I was soon told—in accented but easily understandable German—that

165

she came from the eastern town of Lemberg, where she had been a school teacher.

"One day they came to me," she said, "and told me that I had to leave as quickly as possible. I left—we all left, who did not want to be occupied by the Soviets—and I wandered about with my small child and dit not know where to go. No money, no home, nothing! Then I came here. I have been working at this pump for the past eleven years. What a life!"

After a pause, the woman continued:

"Look at me—I still have no money, and I still have no place which I can call my home! I own a single dress, and I have hardly enough money for my child and myself. You know, the world is insane. They threw people out here, people who were at home in this place. And us—us they threw out of our homes and forced us to settle here! They are playing football with us!"

Then she looked at Jacqueline, and there were tears in her eyes as she raised her hands. "Look," she said, and with a single sentence one woman told another about her desperate condition: "look at my hands, —my hands!"

From a church across the river—a severely damaged church, it was, —came the sound of bells. We were reminded of time, of the need to go on, to see and hear more. Would time also cure the hurt in this woman's body and soul?

On the road to Guben.—After a drive through a beautiful forest we reached *Ziebingen* (Cybinka), a small town which gave us pleasure because we found no ruins there; although many houses were as neglected as those of countless other communities, some actually looked quite well-kept. After what we had seen earlier today, every white-washed wall was a welcome change.

But pleasant impressions are short-lived here. After Ziebingen we again saw steppe-like fallow fields. At frequent intervals there were deep hollows in the highway which were probably due to a weakening of the roadbed; it was hard to spot them from afar and we considered ourselves lucky not to have broken the springs of the car. Warning signs are as rare in these parts as highway repairs.

We had originally intended to drive first to Krossen and then to Guben. But when we came to a sign indicating a direct side road to Guben, which would save us several miles, we decided to take it. The side road could not be much worse than the roll-and-pitch of the main road.

Apart from being narrow and dusty, the secondary road proved quite acceptable. Again we passed "Potemkian Fields"—narrow strips of wheat, rye and oats, planted around the edges of the fields. Then we saw what seemed to be a huge area of feed-grain; the crop looked very well, but when we stopped and checked more closely, we discovered that in this instance the strip around the field was not even three feet wide. It was extraordinary, for even sowing this narrow strip around such a large piece of land must have entailed much work; if there was a shortage of seed, why was so much effort spent sowing a fringe around such a large area, when a small field, thoroughly sown, could be much more efficiently worked?

Further along the road we came across two men who certainly had not worked on the big field or anywhere else. It was five o'clock in the afternoon and the two were totally drunk. They stood in the middle of the road, gesticulating furiously. They looked so wild, that I was determined not to stop. I sounded the horn continuously and in the last moment they staggered aside. In the next village the road led down an incline, to the bank of a river—and there it ended. We checked our maps, found that we had reached the Oder and that there was no bridge anywhere for miles around. Nice short-cut to Guben! we told ourselves.

But soon people began to wave to us and to point to a place on the shore, where a ferry was moored. Fine, we thought,—until we had a closer look at the craft: it was a rickety raft of ancient vintage, with an equally aged crew of ferrymen. It seemed more than doubtful that this contraption of old boards and battered oil drums could support our car across the broad river. I was on the point of turning around, but then—it was a long way back to the cross roads and the old men continued to wave to us, so we crossed our fingers and drove onto the ferry. The ramp to the craft consisted of two narrow, moist planks, and we nearly landed in the Oder before we got aboard, but at last we made it, to the delight of a large audience which had gathered meanwhile. The ferry was hardly longer than the car, nor was its seaworthiness improved by the embarkation of a dozen men who suddenly decided to cross with us; the good ship developed a considerable list to port. Then we cast off: a rope emerged from the green waters, and the ancient worthies, their hands wrapped in canvass, pulled and heaved us across. Our course was not what we had expected: it led us further down-river than towards the opposite shore and we were certain we would arrive in Stettin one of these days. But no one else seemed to be concerned and, after a circuitous route, we finally reached the other side.

Now we have recovered from this little adventure and are continuing on our way to Guben.

Guben.—Like Frankfurt-an-der-Oder, this town, now called Gubin, is a divided city: half of it lies in the DDR, half is under Polish administration.

A few minutes ago we drove up to the Polish border point, without having realized how far we had advanced. We were almost checked out there, and then could have crossed the river Neisse on a new bridge and—had we had a visa—entered the DDR. It is easy to lose one's way here, for all the streets look alike, lined with rubble and ruins; the bridge and a nearby city hall are the only new pieces of construction we could see in Polish Guben. The severely damaged steeple and the burned-out nave of the late-gothic Parish church reach into the sky, like sinister landmarks in a place of death and decay. The eastern part of the town, which stretches up a hill-side, in the direction of Krossen, is particularly depressing; it looks as if this once was a residential district of villas in private gardens; today only hazelnut bushes thrive there, covering stunted walls and other left-overs.

Guben is said to be one of the main border-crossing points for emigrants to the DDR and the West; here they have a symbolic last view of their home-land. For us too, Guben is a typical reminder of the dreadful nothing which prevails here.

From the nothing back to the neutral,—to our over-night headquarters in Stettin.

En route back to Stettin.—Before *Krossen* which has been renamed Krosno, the road leads through extensive forests; these are not particularly well-kept but the timber is at least not being cut planlessly. Around the saw-mills on the frings of Krossen much wood has been stored, which indicates that this is the center of an active lumber industry.

The town itself looks like most others which have not been totally destroyed: neglected houses fringing a shattered center, where a church, though damaged, is still intact. In Krossen the church is in rather good condition.

Further north there are again countless acres of idle land. Even in forest clearings there are fields, which, as one can see, were ploughed two or three years ago; now the furrows are overgrown with grass and soon all evidence of agricultural activity will have vanished.

In the little village of *Skampe,* which is now called Skape, the inhabitants look like gypsies, reminding of those in Pyritz. The fields surrounding the village have not been worked for years. It is hard to imagine how these people earn their livelihood—certainly not from the land. Skampe shows no signs of destruction with the exception of a few larger houses which probably belonged to "kulaks".

Night is falling. We are passing through a broad and apparently uninhabited plain. The highway is good and we are driving fast. Jacqueline is bringing her diary up to date.

The deserted plains, which have also become a form of nothingness, have blended with the darkened sky. Several hours of driving lie ahead before we will reach Stettin, the Neutral Town.

"I WANT TO DIE AT HOME"

On the way to Silesia.—After returning to Stettin yesterday evening, we went to the dining-room of the hotel and, although it was late, still managed to get something to eat. This was made possible because the waiter who served us not only had sympathy for our hungry condition, but also worked with the speed of lightning; in no time he had bought us everything we had ordered and then hovered around our table ready to dash off to the kitchen again, should we require anything else. Moreover, he astonished us by his linguistic skill: he spoke fluent English, French and German. In answer to my questions —he was too polite and reserved to volunteer any information unless he was asked directly—he explained that he was what he called a "foreign Pole" and had spent most of his life in western countries. He had returned home only a short time ago and said he had no complaints about the way he was living here.

"The salaries are not very high," he said, "but since Gomulka one can earn quite a bit of extra money, you know, tips and things. Oh yes, since Gomulka everything has improved. Was a time," he went on, lowering his voice a little, "when everything was better in America. And by 'America' I mean the country to the east of us. It was always being held up as paradise on earth and so we came to call it 'the second America'. But now we've been given a little bit of breathing space, 'paradise' isn't so close anymore. And that's good for us."
The speedily served evening meal was also good for us, we managed to get to bed at a reasonable hour and are able to continue today feeling much refreshed.

First we passed through Pyritz again, but did not stop this time. Then, instead of turning west at Soldin and heading towards the Oder we continued south-east, in the direction of Landsberg-an-der-Warthe. Again we saw much fallow land and fields which were gradually turning into sandy wastes. There is almost no traffic here. A little while ago a lorry came towards us on the left side of the road; when the driver finally saw us he was so astonished he nearly went into the ditch.

A few minutes ago, two and a half miles north of Landsberg, we saw a large former estate which has been turned into a collective.

Just now, on entering Landsberg, we are passing extensive barracks of the Polish army.

Further notes to follow, after we've passed through here.

Later.—*Landsberg an der Warte* (Gorzow Wlkp.) is still a large city, but it is doubtful whether the former population of 46,000 has been reached again. This used to be what official guide books called the "cultural center" of East Brandenbrug. Today it is a particularly dirty industrial town. In the center of the city many—though by no means all—houses have been destroyed. The area around what was once the "Markt", the market, has suffered a lot, but the late-gothic protestant St. Mary's Church, which is in that part of town, is in fairly good condition.

Although this is still a city, the life of its people is nonetheless very primite: a minimum of goods is for sale in the shops, traffic in the streets consists almost exclusively of horse-drawn carts. Moments ago, while we were parked on a street by the river, one horse shied so vehemently that its driver had the greatest difficulty avoiding an involuntary bath in the Warthe for himself and the animal.

Again en route.—*In Schwerin* (Skwierzyna) there is an interesting looking church with a bell-tower separated from the main building, in the Italian campanile style. The church shows no signs of war-time damage and is rather well kept. But the center of the little town is in poor shape; many houses have vanished.

It is noteworthy that in these towns there are still a few reminders of human individuality: if the inhabitants are ready to make some efforts, the utter gloom can be at least partially dispelled. We are looking at such an exemple of local improvement here in Schwerin: on the former site of a house all the rubble has been removed, the burnt black earth dug up and turned into a large flower bed on which countless many-coloured pansies are in full bloom. It may only be a little thing, but what a pleasant sight it is, amidst all this destruction and neglect!

Meseritz is now called Miedzyrzecz, and there is little damage to be seen here. We drove to the main square, the "Marktplatz", stopped and took photographs. While I was working I heard a woman's voice, speaking German behind me.

"My goodness! Just look at that car!"

I turned around and saw two woman—one probably in her sixties, the other much younger—lost in contemplation of our car. I walked towards them and while the younger one continued her silent inspection, her grey-haired companion and I began to chat. It was she whose exclamation I had heard. Now she continued:

"Oh, I tell you, that would be something for my son! If he could only see that car!"

The woman came from Berlin. She was, she told me, the widow of a native of Meseritz.

"After the war we were in Berlin," she recalled. "And suddenly my husband said: 'let's go to Meseritz. I want to die at home.' And so we came here, wretches that we are. And believe it or not a short time later my husband became sick and it wasn't long before he died. His wish was fulfilled, while our life,—well . . . you can see for yourself what it's like. Now I am here with my two sons. We manage to get by."

"How do you manage?" I asked.

"Well, we have a private enterprise," the woman replied. "We came here with two cars—and now we use them as taxis. My sons are the drivers. Of course, the cars are quite old by now and one of them is always in for repairs. Oh, I'll tell you, the boys should see your car—they'd turn green with envy; we'll never get a new model like that."

I asked whether the mother and sons planned to emigrate.

"Oh goodness, we'd like to go! I even have a married daughter in the Federal Republic. But I wouldn't want to become a burden to my daughter's family, and meanwhile the boys are working here, so we're able to make our way. One only has to become accustomed to the dirt; and that isn't easy. The boys don't find it as hard as I do. They've learned a little Polish. But I won't ever learn the language now, that is certain—I am too old. But, well," she concluded with a sigh, "at least we have enough to eat."

"But we never have enough money!" the younger woman added. The hypnotic hold our car had had on her seemed to have been broken. "And we are still Germans, that is certain. Just to be able to see that car there, and the elegant lady in it—that will have to be food for us, for our memories, for a long time. We have nothing else to keep us going."

"Oh don't say such things! It isn't that bad," the older woman countered.

"Oh yes, it is that bad!" her companion said with emphasis, and slowly, as if lost in thought again, she walked away.

The grey-haired one shook her head. "Oh, these young people—they're always complaining," she said.

"I have a feeling that you are not satisfied yourself," I said.

"Well, 'satisfied' is hardly the right expression here, but—oh well—what should one say?" And then she added: "In our little town things go particularly badly, because the state shops only receive those goods which are left over in the bigger cities. Then, when one goes to Stettin or to Danzig, as I did a while ago, then one realizes how good life can be."

Since we had so recently been to Stettin and Danzig, her comparisons enabled me to imagine what life in Meseritz was like.

When I raised my camera to take a picture of the woman, she began to run away.

"My goodness, the things that can happen to you around here!" she exclaimed as she fled. "Soon this will also be just like the big cities!"

What a metropolis was really like had evidently become a blurred memory to her. And why not?

It is easy for one's recollections to become hazy here. Dull greyness reaches into all aspects of life, casting a pall, flattening, crushing everything in the process of reduction to the lowest common denominator. Conditions may sometimes vary from place to place, contrasts may be found here and there, but these are minimal.

Schwiebus, now called Swiebodzin, is one of those places with minor differences in conditions. We have just passed through the town and noticed that hardly any houses were damaged. The imposing steeple of the city hall was unharmed. The shops in one street were stocked with more than the usual variety of merchandize. But here too the all-embracing greyness soon appeared:

We stopped at a restaurant in order to buy a few bottles of mineral water for our lunch. There was none to be had. But there was vodka in vast quantities and countless consumers of this refreshment, who had evidently been busy for some time, keeping the restaurant's sales figures at an impressive level—in other words: the place was filled with drunks.

As we were about to continue, the car was again surrounded by the usual crowd—among them several drunken men. The greyness had closed in. Even the people were grey; it was if they did not live, but merely existed, as if all their surroundings were of equal indifference to them, as if they knew that only vodka could help them to attain some temporary relief, some temporary gaiety.

The environment in which these people exist, the devastated houses and those in varying stages of collapse, the fallow land, the plains turning into steppe—all this cannot find even temporary escape in vodka. Inevitably the all-pervading greyness becomes increasingly intense. Thereupon the people who have been compelled to live on this land, react in their turn to the gathering darkness, the stifling hopelessness about them, and tend the more to seek comfort in alcohol. It is a vicious circle.

174

The only people exempt from this diabolical trap set for the human soul are the few original inhabitants of this land, who have remained behind. And what is happening to them? Their recollections become hazy—in fact they themselves become vaguely defined, blurred shadows of another age.

DANZIG. Above, two of its best known buildings: at right, the ruin of the »Krantor«, a famous old storage elevator, and center, the St. Mary's Church (Marienkirche). Both are being rebuilt exactly as they were. Church and state are jointly financing the rebuilding of St. Mary's, the latter having undertaken the exterior, the former the interior work. The picture below was taken from the same location before the war.

Danzig is being rebuilt in the style which once made this hanseatic town famous. But few immediately tangible mementos of the german population are to be found. Where these still exist, they usually take the form of signs and inscriptions on ruins.

Despite the great reconstruction effort many parts of Danzig are still in ruins. At some places we found only street signs in polish, where the rebuilding programme had not yet begun.

Mr. Lech Kadlubowski (above) is the chief architect of the Danzig reconstruction programme. He is a native of Wilna, in russian-occupied eastern Poland. He never saw Danzig before it was destroyed. Beside enthusiasm for his work, he can draw on an immense store of documentation about every detail of the town's pre-war appearance, which, in turn, has made possible the construction of a scale model of the old town (below).

Three stages of reconstruction in Danzig are to be seen here: above, the rear view of houses recently built in the old style, but with facades not yet decorated. They face the former »Hundegasse«. In the foreground, a field of rubble with some piled bricks where another block of houses will be erected later. The »Hundegasse« is a parallel street to the famous »Lange Markt«, the completely rebuilt houses of which are seen in the picture below.

The newly reconstructed »Steffensche Haus«, one of the patrician houses on the »Lange Markt«, is an excellent example of the faithful way in which the old facades are being recreated. All these houses had been completely destroyed. Some Poles deny the style of these buildings is German, others are more concerned with the rebuilding of architectural monuments, no matter what their origin.

Two other famous landmarks of Danzig have been rebuilt: the »Neptune Fountain« on the »Lange Markt« and the city hall with its massive tower.

GDYNIA. Poland's only port between the two wars, looked prosperous. We saw more goods in the shops, better dressed people and there was more traffic in the streets than in most other cities.

LAUENBURG. Apart from a few bombed buildings in the center of the town, Lauenburg showed very little damage. The proximity of the pre-war german polish border may have had something to do with this, saving the town from soviet revenge actions which began further west. The banderolle across the street, with its propaganda phrases is typical for all communist countries.

STOLP. The center of the city is completely shattered (above). The business section of town was in the foreground. The »Garnison-Church« in the background was not too seriously damaged. To the left of the church, the remains of the castle. Below: the least damage in Stolp was to be found around the soviet war memorial, which was well-kept and surrounded by flower beds.

The western city gate of Stolp is well preserved. Beyond it lies the shattered business section. From here we drove north to the Baltic Sea coast before continuing further west in the direction of Stettin.

Between Stolp and Schlawe we saw much fallow land, some of which was turning into a wild steppe. The seeds of the trees growing in the foreground were driven by the wind from woodlots on the horizon, planted years ago as windbreaks for what was then valuable farm land.

SCHLAWE. As is so often the case, the heart of the city of Schlawe lies in ruins while the church, in the very center, has miraculously escaped total destruction. This church, however, lost the top half of its spire.

KÖSLIN is another provincial capital which is said to have more inhabitants today than it did in german times. A good deal of construction is under way, but the work progresses slowly, partly because of the lack of modern machines, partly because the effect of Poland's greatest social enemy, vodka, is everywhere in evidence.

KOLBERG. The well-known Baltic seaside resort has become an eerie ghost-town. Above: the skeleton-like remains of a resort hotel near the beach. Below: the completely deserted beach in front of the hotel shown above.

The middle of Kolberg was hardly to be found. This picture shows an area which probably was the center. In the background at left, the remains of Kolberg's well-known St. Mary's Church (Marienkirche).

CAMMIN IN POMERANIA. Wherever we went we saw destroyed industrial concerns which were apparently not destined to be rebuilt. In Cammin we came across what must have been an large brewery.

In the middle of Cammin a stretch of desert had developped. In the center, the remains of the city hall; in the background, right, the damaged tower of the church.

STETTIN. Approaching the center of this formerly large and important metropolis, one passes street-corners such as the one shown on this picture. Amid empty
spaces stand burnt-out houses, exactly as they were destroyed in 1945. Rats, cats,
and stray dogs haunt these houses and at the corners shattered lights hang at strange
angles; it all looks like a surrealistic drawing, but is reality.

As I photographed these sad remains of Stettin's Jakobi Church, a Pole assured me this was the »St. Paula Church«. The new inhabitants of Stettin have, naturally enough, no intellectual or emotional ties to this town and are not even interested in the names of its important landmarks. This lack of interest intensifies the grey, neutral impression the town makes.

These pictures were both made from a street (the »Kleine Domstrasse«) which once led through a densely built-up area. Now nothing stands between the street and the estuary of the Oder which lies beyond the ruins in the picture above. The damaged castle of Stettin (below), was invisible from this street before the war.

Only very few famous structures are being repaired in Stettin, among them the Berlin Gate, the »Berliner Tor«. Below left, a picture of the gate as it once looked. Above, its present condition. In the foreground lie the decorative stone sections which were knocked off during the war. They are now being repaired and will be remounted on the gate.

The »Neue Rathaus«, the new city hall of Stettin, has been left exactly as it was in 1945: a burnt-out shell. Nothing has been done to prevent the building from collapsing.

Some streets of Stettin show far less damage, and once in a while one still has the feeling of being in a large town. There are more goods in the shops and one sees a few people who are fairly well-dressed.

Ruins and half-shattered houses in what once was a street in Stettin.

In a residential area around the former Kaiser-Wilhelm-square, the visitor sees normal conditions. Only the absence of traffic seems unusual. The stripes on the building are flags.

New houses are being constructed in Stettin. Above: a block of flats which will have shops on the ground floor. Below, a better looking building in a purely residential district. It is customary for tenants to move in long before the building is completed.

PYRITZ. The picture at left shows a street in the old walled city of Pyritz as it once looked. The tower belonged to the northern gate. We searched for more than an hour, using an old city plan and checking carefully, before we could find the same spot as it looks today (below). Apart from ruins such as this, nothing remains of the old part of Pyritz.

The eastern gate of Pyritz stands in part. The section of city wall to the right of the tower is one of the few remaining pieces of what once was the best preserved specimen of its kind in this area.

SOLDIN. Only one of the two city gates of this little town was to be found, the other had vanished. On the gate we saw russian letters which may be an abreviation for the name of the communist party of Poland.

KÜSTRIN. The destruction in the center of Küstrin was one of the worst impressions of our journey. Even ruins are rare here.

FRANKFURT AN DER ODER. The polish portion of Frankfurt looks like a small provincial town: it consists of a few streets with neglected houses. A larger part of the town is on the opposite shore of the Oder, and hence in the Soviet Zone of Germany.

On the way from Frankfurt to Guben, we crossed the Oder by ferry. It was a craft of doubtful seaworthiness, which followed an uneasy course across the river, guided by an ancient ferryman and some equally aged helpers.

GUBEN. Like Frankfurt, Guben is also a town divided between the Soviet Zone of Germany and Poland. This picture shows the trees and bushes which have spread over the ruins on the polish side. Beyond them, the roofs and the church steeple in the Soviet sector.

In the polish part of Guben almost all buildings are damaged or destroyed. The burnt-out steeple of the late-gothic parish church looks like a gigantic gravestone in this cemetary of a former town.

KROSSEN. This town resembles countless other communities in these territories which have escaped total destruction: neglected houses, a razed central area and in the middle, a church which, although damaged, still stands.

Between Stettin and Landsberg an der Warthe we again saw considerable areas of fallow land. In part, these fields have been neglected so long that they are about to become a desert.

LANDSBERG AN DER WARTHE is still a rather large town. Once it was considered the cultural center of East Brandenburg; today it's a dirty industrial city. Here too the center of the town is full of gaping holes, particularly around the market square. But the late-gothic protestant St. Mary's Church, the tower of which is seen in the background, has survived.

In Landsberg, as in most cities through which we drove, traffic consisted chiefly of horse-drawn carts. The horse seen in this picture was so frightened by our car that its driver had the greatest difficulty saving himself and the horse from an involuntary bath in the river Warthe, which flows just beyond the railing.

MESERITZ. This unusually well-kept park in the middle of Meseritz struck us as a sensation after the experiences of the previous days. On the outskirts of the town some buildings had been bombed or burnt.

We met this old woman, a native of Berlin, in Meseritz. She had come to the small town at the end of the war because her husband, born and raised there, had wanted to die at home. He had died, and now her sons opperate two old cars as private taxis. The woman did not like to be photographed. »Soon this will also be like the big cities!« she exclaimed as she ran away.

Everywhere during our trip we noticed how many young men always seemed to have time to gather around our car and to discuss its technical data. They came at all hours of the day, always fairly well dressed and in good physical condition. They often looked better off than factory workers, but could not be students, for there were no holidays at this time.

SCHWIEBUS. This town was another of the pleasant exceptions during our journey. The shops in this street were well stocked with more than the usual variety of merchandize. The interesting-looking steeple of the city hall was unharmed.

SILESIA

"SO DANGEROUS, BUT SO LOVELY!"

Grünberg.—She wore black. She looked at me with sad eyes. "You are knowing what it is, a bad life?" she asked. "I think I do," I replied. "Then please, you multiply with a hundred, and then you are having the life of us." As she said this, the face of the Polish woman speaking to me in broken German showed me that she was certain I could not possibly understand her, could never imagine what "bad multiplied with a hundred" really meant. Perhaps she was right. Nor did she attempt any further explanation, but greeted me politely and went on her way. The woman was one of the many people who have crowed around us here in what is now called Zielona Gora, not only to stare at us, as is usually the case, but also talk to us.

Thus we soon gained the impression that Grünberg's population is more talkative and livelier than elsewhere, even if the things they say are not too cheerful. But after the graveyards of cities which are behind us, even this is certainly a welcome change. And the positive impression is not limited to the population: we have also noticed that there is relatively little war-time damage, and that buildings laid low by bombs or granades are being reconstructed. Many blocks of houses are untouched, particularly in that part of the town where there are large former residences and villas; these, as is customary, now serve either as club-houses, office buildings or have been converted into five or more flats per house.

Wherever we stopped during our trip through Grünberg—and we did this frequently—the many talkative people came to us. Like the sad woman already mentioned, most of them were Poles, confirming again what we had already noted: it is not only the few remaining Germans who complain about life in these territories.

An elderly man who, judging by his overalls, was perhaps a mason, came close to me and whispered:

"The West, first rate, Poland . . .!" and he used an unprintable word.

A young man and a pretty young woman—probably a newly married couple, asked whether we had connections to the American embassy in Warsaw and might help them get an immigrant's visa to th USA. Shortly thereafter a well-dressed man about forty years old, offered me 7,000 Zloty for the spare tire of our car. He explained that he had bought an American car some years ago, but could not use it any more because the tires were worn out.

I regretted that we could not possibly sell our spare tires (we even have an second one with us, in order to avoid the danger of being marooned somewhere) and asked whether the man was sure that my size of tire would fit his car.

"Are there different sizes?" he asked, showing great surprise. "I thought all American cars were alike!" Now he seemed glad that I had not accepted his offer right away; 7,000 Zloty, seven times the amount of an average monthly wage in Poland and, at the artificial exchange rate for foreigners about 208 Dollars, would have been quite a price for a used spare tire which might not even fit the car.

"I would pay much, much more for a new car," the man said. "But to get one of those Wartburgs from East Germany, or a Russian car, you have to wait for years."

I decided to put a direct question to the man:

"You must have a very important position to be able to spend so much money."

He shrugged his shoulders. "There is always money if one knows what to do," he said. He did not stay with me much longer after that.

We stopped near a "Delikatesy" shop, planning to buy fresh supplies. Jacqueline left to make the purchases while I remained behind to mount guard and take some pictures. She stayed away a long time and when she finally got back I was ready to deliver myself of a few well-chosen words about females who always dawdle in shops. But Jacqueline took the wind out of my sails before I could say anything. "Drive on," she said, "and give me my diary, "I have some interesting things to write."

Herewith her notes:

Am in "Delikatesy," in quest of fruit juice and tins of fish. "Delikatesy" very dark, which complicates quest, but facilitates conspiratory scene with sinister lady.

Self-same slinks up to me without my noticing her, and gently touches my shoulder. I howl, not being addicted to shoulder-touching in gloomy "Delikatesy". Other shadowy tin purchasers turn around, while sinister lady looks innocent and goes into bored nose-powdering act. After other customers have forgotten my howl, bored powdering-act ceases. Sinister lady once again slinks up to me.

She is between thirty and forty years old, has black dress with white spots and white face with black spots. Not beautiful. But very cunning —apart from being sinister.

Favours me with cunning-sinister grin and whispers:

"You have perhaps Dollars what is to be sold?"

Little light blinks within me: black market! black market is forbidden, forbidden things have way of leading one to militia, militia has way of leading one to jail, jail has way of requiring unwanted separation from cameraman-reporter-husband. Shake head wisely. Have no Dollars. Further dialogue between sinister lady (hereinafter referred to as S.L.) and me (referred to as J.W.) as follows:

S.L.: *But surely you have Dollars! Make wonderful business with you. 130 Zloty for one Dollar.*
(Must add: official rate, 24 Zloty per Dollar.)
J.W.: *I have no Dollars and if I had some, I know it is forbidden to change them privately.*
S.L.: *Of course is forbidden. But business I make with you is good. Who asks if is forbidden?*
J.W.: *I do!*
S.L.: *Oh—is great mistake you are making.—But then perhaps you will sell purse perhaps?*
J.W.: *No.*
S.L.: *Is so dangerous, but so lovely!*
J.W.: *(She's telling me!) Exactly, that's why I don't wish to . . .*
S.L.: *But you sell something, no?*
J.W.: *No.*
S.L.: *Yes!*
J.W.: *No! I have already told you that I have absolutely nothing for sale. Now please leave me alone.*
S.L.: *Oh—is much a pity. You wish not to become rich! We in Poland have such good way to becoming rich.*
She departs, shaking her head. Buy my tins after much groping about in dark shop. Finally reach daylight again, and who stands before me? Sinister lady!
Once more gives me full treatment with cunning-sinister grin.
"No Dollars? no purse? no nothing?" she asks. "So dangerous—but so lovely!"
Decide this time reply is superfluous and return to car and bad-tempered Charles.

The preceeding diary entries were written during our current stop at a gasoline pump in Grünberg. We have to wait. A tank-truck belonging to the state gasoline company is delivering fuel at the pump and all sales of gasoline have come to a halt. We have been told that there is only this one pump in Grünberg. So we have no choice but to wait.

The people are not only very friendly hereabouts, they also speak remarkably fluent German. We assume that this has something to do with the part of eastern Poland from which the new population of this town has come. There were certain areas in the east, for instance those which once were part of the Austro-Hungarian empire, where much German was spoken.

The filling station attendant is also one of those who speak fluent German. He greeted us most politely and promised that we would not have to wait very long.

Later one of the attendant's helpers came to us. He was a blond and blue-eyed man of about thirty years. He marched up to my window and yelled at me in a German riminiscent of a Prussian army sergeant: "Tell me—can't you put yourself any place else? Can't you see that you're creating an uproar just because you're standing right here, so near the pump? Never seen anyone quite so inconsiderate as you in all my life!"

"Well, well, calm down, won't you?" I replied, "I'm only waiting to fill up at your pump."

"You'll have to wait another two hours," the man yelled back at me. "And in the meantime you're blocking all the traffic here and making trouble for us!"

It was true that a crowd of fifty or sixty people had gathered around the car again, but otherwise there was no "traffic" which we could possibly have blocked.

"Alright, where do you want me to park?" I asked in order to end his yelling, wondering the while who this extraordinary fellow might be.

His next order was already forthcoming:

"Over there! park over there in the side street! hard against the kerb! and be quick about it!"

I am still furious at myself for being so mild with him. I drove to the place he had indicated, and here we are now, still waiting. But all is well—here comes the nice attendant. We can drive over and fill up. The whole delay dit not last more than a quarter of an hour, and it's

213

been three minutes and not two hours since the sergeant-helper made his pompous appearance.

Later.—We are only around the corner from the service station, because we have halted again, in order to note the rest of our experiences there:

I drove to the pump, where the pleasant attendant was already waiting for me, hose in hand. The supply truck was still pumping gasoline into the station's tanks, so that it looked as if the attendant was making a special effort to provide us with fuel—perhaps to make up for the bad manners displayed by his helper.

There being no electric pumps at the station, (they hardly exist anywhere in Poland) the sergeant-helper now had to pump back and forth, five liters at a time, until our tank was filled. Meanwhile he was yelling just as violently as before—this time in Polish, at some of the people standing around us.

An older man in plus-fours and a tattered jacket came to me and, with every sign of disapproval, pointed at the sergeant:

"He's got a real big trap, hasn't he," he said in accent-free German.

"Is he a German?" I asked.

"Yes, of course!" the man told me.

"And he's allowed to put on an act like this?" I exclaimed, still thinking of the way I had been treated.

"Sure, his kind gets away with anything," was the reply.

"How is it that he speaks fluent Polish too?" I inquired.

"He learned it. That sort has to." The man said with a shrug.

"How do you mean?"

"He's one of those who like to crawl to the winning side—I'm sure you know the type. He's into everything, wriggles his way in and then puffs himself up. Oh yes, we have that kind here—not many, thank God, but still, enough."

"And you? You're German too?" I asked.

"That I am! But I don't crawl, believe me," the man said and gave the object of his dislike a hate-filled look.

I entered the station attendant's office to pay my bill.

Outside a verbal battle had broken out between the sergeant-helper and the onlookers. The attendant, a good-looking young man, smiled wearily and to my astonishment, spoke to me in English:

"I hope you didn't have to wait too long," he said politely.

I assured him the delay had not been great and went on to ask him where he had learned to speak English.

"At university," the attendant replied. "Yes, I can see, you are surprised, but such a thing can happen quite easily with us. I studied medicine, and one day they came and fetched me away."

"Who were 'they'?"

"The UB, the secret police. I was given six years at hard labour. I am only free for the past year."

Now, looking at him closely, I noticed that he had a nervous tick in his face. Perhaps it had been brought on by his recollections of the past.

"Why were you sentenced?" I asked.

"The charge was: illegal possession of a firearm," the attendant replied.

"And did you have a weapon?"

"Yes, I had to have it to defend myself—unfortunately. But if I had not had one, they would have found another reason for arresting me. They wanted to have me out of the way."

"Why?"

"I was an organizer of catholic youth groups. That was one of the worst crimes one could commit in those days." And once again his face twitched noticeably.

"And now, how is the situation now?" I went on to ask.

He hesitated before he replied: "Who knows? better—but for how long? one hopes, one prays."

Outside, the sergeant-helper continued to behave in character. Jacqueline was destined to become his next victim. But this time he had miscalculated: I returned in time to witness a scene which gladdened my heart.

Jacqueline had lit a cigarette in the car, an error which she does not deny. But instead of pointing out the oversight, the self-important man rushed up to her and screamed:

"What do you think you are doing? Where were you taught things like that? In Germany you are not allowed to do such a thing—smoking in front of a gasoline station!"

Jacqueline extinguished her cigarette and gave the sergeant a friendly smile: "We are not in Germany," she said, "but in the People's Republic of Poland".

The sergeant was confused, but evidently decided that the best defence lay in another attack.

"You want to blow us all up, don't you?" he yelled.

"It wouldn't be a bad idea—if only you were to go up," Jacqueline replied in a positively sweet tone and continued to smile amiably.

We drove away, leaving behind us an—at least temporarily—subdued sergeant-helper and an applauding multitude.

We are now about to drive once more through Zielona Gora—incidentally this is another capital of a wojewodztwo or province—to make a short side-trip to a place called Rothenburg-an-der-Oder.

Rothenburg-an-der-Oder.—We came here, to find out if what we had heard is true: that there are settlements of "Repatrianten" here, people recently repatriated to Poland after years spent as prisoners or internees in the Soviet Union. It had originally been disclosed in Warsaw that some repatriated Poles had been brought to camps here and in other parts of the country, but later announcements indicated that the camps had been virtually dissolved; the repatriated Poles, many of whom were said to be Jews, were declared to have been absorbed into the normal life of the country. We were interested to see to what extent and with what measure of success this action had been carried out.

Rothenburg, now Czerwiensk, turned out to be a sleepy village with equally sleepy inhabitants. I tried the word "Repatrianten" on several citizens, but it did not seem to mean anything to them. Finally we found someone who could speak German and were told that a camp or repatriation center was located less than two miles from the village. We are now parked before the entrance to the camp. It looks like a converted army installation or perhaps a former internment or prison camp. Over the entrance there is the inscription: "Punkt Repatriacyjny". There is no sign of guards; a gatekeeper is asleep in a small sentry hut. Inside the camp some people walk up and down and outside the stockade a few old men and women sit by the roadside. A woman, hunched and wrinkled by age, sitting on a mile-stone near-by, has not taken her eyes off us since we arrived. She is staring at us, as if we were ghosts.

Some small children are running around the car. We have noted that all of them have clean-shaven heads—boys and girls alike—reminiscent of russian children. Or perhaps these unfortunate ones have spent their entire lives in camps, where precautions must always be taken to protect them from vermin?

The children speak a language we neither understand nor recognize. It certainly is not Polish, and we doubt whether it is Russian. Perhaps a form of Yiddish.

CHILDREN, RUSSIANS AND A SANDSTORM

Christianstadt.—Once upon a time there was a little child who had many, many toys. Although it was naughty and above all argumentative, ever bent on taking other children's toys away from them, one thing had to be said about this child: it always kept its toys in good order, seeing to it that everything was spotless and that nothing ever broke down. One day a great fight developed and the child who had so much was severely beaten by the others and during the course of the fight also lost many of its toys. One of the children in the neighbourhood managed to get most of the lost toys, although only after they had been badly scratched, and in some cases even broken. Once peace had been restablished, the victorious child which had captured so much, insisted on keeping the toys. And because so much had been damaged or broken, it took what money it had saved and had some toys repaired. For these repairs the child chose the oldest among the captured things, objects which were very pretty but quite useless, because they were too old by now, and because the victorious child really needed altogether different things at this stage in its development.

But soon all the available money was spent and thus there was no further way of having the right toys repaired. Thereupon the victorious but impecunious child complained bitterly, it even shed tears, but to no avail; at last it invented a new game which could be played without toys. The game was called "possum"—named after the animal which lies down and pretends to be dead when it is in danger, hoping that the danger will soon pass. It was a dull and unproductive game, but the child did not know what else it might do . . .

One invents such malicious fables when visiting Christianstadt and *Naumburg,* two communities in the former province of East Branden-burg. We had already crossed into Silesia north of Grünberg, but re-entered East Brandenburg for this visit. Christianstadt is now called Krzywaniec, Naumburg Nowogrod. Here there are many "toys": they are the numerous factories located in this area. And the "children" of my fable: Germany and Poland. The superannuated toy,—Danzig,— is being repaired at great cost to the victorious "child", but the other "playthings"—these factories—are left to lie idle, bombed, burned out and neglected. In Naumburg we saw two or three factories in this condition. Here, in Christianstadt there is a large establishment which used to belong to the huge chemical trust, I. G. Farben; it consists of a big factory and a housing development for the workers. Not a soul is in sight here. The homes and the factory buildings, not even severely damaged in this instant, are gradually collapsing. The only indication that people ever come to this place is a small wheat field, planted where the former road leading to the chemical plant must have been. I can make out a stork's nest on the top of the factory chimney.

But the child complains because it has no toys, and plays "possum". We ask ourselves: how can such things be? Then we take pictures of the broken "toys", shake our heads and continue on our way.

Sagan (Zagan).—Often we regret, that we did not know this country as it once was and must base our comparison on old photographs and travel books. But occasionally this lack of experience has its beneficial side; this is the case here in Sagan.

There is a famous chateau here which dates from the 17th century and has an interesting history: in 1844 it was bought by the Talley-rand family and remained in the hands of the famous French minister's heirs until the beginning of the second world war. We travelled here chiefly in order to visit this chateau and to find out in what condition it might be. But, not knowing our way around this town, we spent some time trying to locate the ducal seat, and thus saw more of the city and spoke to more people than we might ordinarily have done.

At first we could not find our way at all nor did we encounter any one who could help, for the entire town seemed to be peopled only by men in uniform,—motorized soldiers who sped through Sagan in all directions. We drove and wandered through the town, noting that the war had left its mark in many places but that the town as a whole had not been completely disfigured. Yet, we had a strange overall impression and sought the adjective that would describe Sagan ade-quately: empty? dead?—no, these were not the right words. After we had continued a little further we decided that we had found the word: bedevilled!

Almost everything that is needed to complete the picture of a town was there, and yet it did not seem right, not real. There were also citizens on hand, as it turned out, not just the military, but they seem-ed to fit here even less than the new settlers we had encountered else-where.

Once we stood on a square where there was less military traffic and wondered why this strangeness was so pronounced and then came the first hint: a man crossed the square pushing a baby-carriage. His torso was bare and the rest of his clothing consisted of a pair of sandals and—pyjama trousers!

Now things began to fall into place: I recalled stories in various weekly illustrated magazines—pictures of holiday resorts on the Black Sea, pictures of the holiday makers on the beach and in the streets of the resort towns, the men wearing the customary clothing for such places: pyjamas! The man with the baby-carriage was a Russian! The many cars, jeeps and other vehicles which were dashing about here belonged to the Red Army. We had reached that part of the former German territories in which the Russian Warsaw Pact Forces were stationed! The strange atmosphere—bedevilment we had called it—was explained: Sagan was a Russian garrison town. If—as is the case—an American military town can seem quite strange in western Europe, how much stranger is the impression made by a Russian city in the formerly German part of Poland!

I continued my walk through the streets and made tests at random: I asked passers-by in German where I might find the chateau. I asked twelve times. Twice I received an answer in accented German. Four times, when I was not understood and then asked: "Polski"? I was given a fluent answer which, although I did not understand it completely, was nonetheless able to identify as being in Polish. Six times the people I questioned—among them two women—shook their heads even when I tried for an answer in "polski".

Returning to the square where we had seen the pyjama-clad Russian I noticed an architecturally fine building which however was beginning to deteriorate. I knew from the old photographs that this was not the ducal chateau and judged the building to be some other chateau or perhaps a bishop's residence. I walked around the building and entered a court-yard in which there was the entrance to a large church. Evening services were in progress. The church was so full that many worshipers knelt outside its doors. It was not the first time that we had seen over-filled churches in Poland. I was fairly certain that the people who had come to pray would more likely be Poles than Russians. To make sure I again decided to accost someone. On the second try I found a man who spoke German.

With a smile he confirmed my thoughts:

"Here everyone is Pole," he said. "The Russians do not pray, they shoot."

As he said this I realized that my question had been superfluous: this was a Roman Catholic Church. The man went on to explain that the building I had first noticed was a monestery and that it contained the oldest astronomical observatory in Poland.

"But this observatory hasn't been in Poland for long," I said wondering how we would react to this.

"Not for long. And who knows how much longer," was his prompt reply. "Also it is not certain how long will the people be allowed to kneel in the front of churches. Nothing is certain here. Believe me. I am a man with experience."

"How do you mean that?"

"Look," he said with a sigh. "I am typical for the uncertainty of which I speak: I am a Jew. You know what I mean? When came here the Germans, they said: 'Dirty Jew!' and they locked me in a concentration camp. This I survived. Then came the Russians and they said to me: 'Dirty capitalist!' and they locked me up. That I also survived. Now I am here and now begin the Poles to sing a song which already my ancestors heard: 'Dirty Jew, get out, get out!' So you see, every thing is not for long.—Not the one, and not the other. This way it is with everything today. It is not nice."

"Is there much anti-semitism here?" I asked.

"Look, has there ever been a time in which was no anti-semitism?" was the resigned reply. And then he added: "But also it is getting worse again and many families of Jews are feeling it and if they can, are going to Israel."

"And you? What are you going to do?"

He shrugged his shoulders. "I have seen enough. Worse it cannot get anymore. I am sitting here, I am waiting."

This man was able to explain clearly where the ducal chateau was, and now we had no trouble finding it.

The search had hardly been worth it. It ended with another dreadful picture of destruction to be added to our ever-growing list. The chateau is still there, that is to say, its walls and roof are there. Nothing much else. One can tell that it must have been a most beautiful building but wonders how it was possible to do it so much harm; the damage obviously does not date from the war, but is the result of continuing vandalism. There is hardly a spot on the walls without a gouged-out hole or a scratch. All windows are broken and inside everything is smashed. Someone went to great trouble to throw into the moat parts of the interior masonry and sections of the stone-work which once decorated entrances and window frames.

The park around the chateau, which must have been very attractive, looks like the courtyard of a slum tenement. Everywhere people lie about on neglected fields which once were formal lawns; the men chiefly dressed in pyjamas trousers, the women wearing something resembling cotton house-coats. Many of the trees in the park have been cut and at several places there are large garbage dumps.

We are sitting on a half-smashed park bench, looking at this gloomy sight. There is nothing to say.—We had better move on before all this depresses us even more.

Sprottau.—A strong wind has been blowing for some time now. There are so many sandy patches and arid spots on the fields that the wind is twisting huge dark clouds into the sky. Our vision is seriously impeded. Sprottau, the next town after Sagan, and now renamed Szprotawa, looked ghostly through these clouds, the steeples of its churches seeming separated from the ground, floating like a mirage. Later, when we reached the town, the ghostliness increased: the streets were filled with sand-clouds as thick as fog and in the many bombed-out lots fiercely twisting columns of sand weaved and danced before they spilled into the streets.

We saw some Russian soldiers but otherwise the streets were deserted.

We drove on, leaving the storm behind, past a huge Russian military encampment heading for Bunzlau where we will meet the Autobahn which connects Berlin and Breslau and several cities further east.

En route to Breslau.—We have already passed three or four large Russian camps and also several big buildings with signs in Russian on them. At intervals Soviet military police cars are parked beside the road.

It is impossible to ignore these sights, inevitable that one thinks of their significance: certainly, one reasons, the Russians are strange to us; they come from the east, they differ from the familiar in their appearance, their characteristics, their way of life; their soldiers deal with human beings in a manner bearing witness to such a different set of values that their very proximity terrifies many people in the west; moreover, the strangeness also stems from another root: like it or not, we are victims of our own propaganda. But even taking all this into consideration, one more factor must be added: occupation force remains occupation force and per se engenders strangeness. No matter whether the occupier comes from the east or the west, whether encamped somewhere as victor or out of political considerations which are camouflaged by an international agreement and decorated with a long and imposing name, in the final analysis it is all the same. The Great Power sits like the drone in the bee-hive, contributing nothing productive to the life of the so-called host-country; the Power is always recognizable by the foreign uniforms of its men, it is a law unto itself and a closed-off community, anti-social, therefore negative, always frightening, always a warning that the small political match-stick inadvertently lit can become a world-embracing conflagration in less time than it takes to cry NATO or Warsaw-Pact. It is this strangeness, the closed-off and threatening atmosphere which one feels again and again when passing the camps and stations, indeed every platoon, belonging to the occupier. And here in these territories, where every moment brings so many reminders of the last war these thoughts and feelings become particularly strong.

We have reached the Autobahn to Breslau. Not long ago Jacqueline and I drove on another Autobahn, the one connecting Karlsruhe and Frankfurt, locked into an apparently endless chain of speeding automobiles while the same amount of traffic roared down the opposite two lanes. Now we are here. What a difference! During the last while we have written a good deal into our diary. Now I am going to turn on the tape-recorder to capture my immediate impressions while driving along here:

It is difficult to imagine a green desert. But there is such a thing. Here it is, on my left as well as my right. It must have been a very pleasant landscape around here—stretches of flat land, then gentle hills, a few deeper valleys then plains again. Here and there in the distance a village, otherwise a region ideally suited for agriculture. And what grows here? Bushes, a little grass and weeds—all this is in the furrows of extensive fields where nothing has been sown. That is the green desert.

Kaplunck, kaplunck, kaplunck—monotonously the car rolls across the concrete blocks of the Autobahn. The four lanes of the super-highway are in excellent condition. And why not? The road was new when the war stifled all traffic. And now, indeed since the end of the war, practically no one drives here. What little traffic there is, is more local then long-distance and consists chiefly of lorries and the cars of officials who drive from one village to another, using the secondary roads. Only the green strip between the two double lanes reminds one of the neglect which prevails here as everywhere else in these territories: the grass on this strip is never mown and now it is beginning to grow between the concrete blocks of the road itself. On the side of the road one sees the first signs of what will probably happen one day: the super-highway will be overgrown.

But now it is still in good condition. A lorry has just passed on the opposite side. Jacqueline is relieved, for this is proof that the road is actually open and does not suddenly come to an end with a missing bridge further along the way. There are few warning signs and so we might indeed have ended this drive with a wild leap through the air. The lorry has a calming effect which will last at least until the next cross-roads.

It is interesting that the Autobahn is not marked as such on our polish map, but merely listed as an ordinary high-way. Perhaps it does come to a sudden end somewhere along the way? One can never be sure. Darkness has fallen. We must be careful.

We've been driving for almost an hour without seeing another vehicle. —At last, relief!—we've just reached the turn-off to the town of Liegnitz. In the autumn 1956 we once drove this far, coming from Breslau. Just after this turn-off we were stopped by some soldiers and turned back.

Both sides of the Autobahn are intact between here and Breslau, that we know. Now I can speed up. Thank God.

"ROCK-'N'-ROLL", WROCLAW VERSION

Breslau.—The Hotel "Monopol" in Breslau is an old acquaintance of ours—a bad old acquaintance. We lived here during our stay in what is now Wroclaw in the autumn of 1956 and found it terrible. It is still terrible.

The reception hall still smells as badly as before. The equally evil-smelling little man with the eunuch's voice and the filthy shirt without a collar is still the night porter. The restaurant with its farm-yard odours, its too loud, bad dance music and the endless delays until the food comes to the tables—always cold—hasn't changed much either. Our room is anything but clean. Several light switches do not function, nor does the toilet in the adjoining bathroom. The beds are very bad. But when one is tired one sleeps anywhere, and we proved it in the past night—during eight hours!

At breakfast-time Jacqueline was ready before me and went ahead down to the dining-room to order our eggs and hot water. We knew from previous experience that it would take at least twenty minutes until something would be brought to the table. When I joined her, Jacqueline was busily writing in her diary and I found the following report.

My arrival in dining-room causes usual flight of all waiters.
All waiters? Silly joke! Both of them! Wait a few minutes, but they fail to return. Minutes can be long when stomach empty. Frame of mind: gloomy.
Then two Polish army officers arrive and sit at next table. Immediately a waiter appears. I croak a friendly "prosze pana!" Waiter unimpressed by the fact I call him "mister", attends exclusively to the two officers. They evidently also have empty stomachs. But their's are to be filled. And how! They're served two orders of ham, two huge glasses of vodka, two gigantic glasses of beer. They drink the vodka with one gulp, sip beer as a chaser, then attack ham.
"Prosze pana!" I croak a little louder. Voice is feeble at this time of morning. Waiter singularly disinterested by "prosze" and "pana", continues on his deliberate way back to kitchen.
Frame of mind: Gloomy, mixed with black.
Officers become animated. Slap each other on the shoulder. Ham eaten, beer has joined vodka. One officer, chap with flowing mustache, bangs with knife on vodka glass. Result magnificent: waiter appears, is given order, ignores me and vanishes. Returns in no time carrying, —yes, that's it: Two orders of ham, two huge glasses of vodka, two gigantic glasses of beer.
I swing into action: take knife from other table, bang lustily against glass from third table. Waiter stares, comes to me. Ask if he speaks French, English, German. Shakes his head. Mutters something about "kolega" and vanishes.
Officers' breakfast continues. Vodka has already disappeared, beer is performing chaser duties, ham is being attacked.
Frame of mind: Gloomy, mixed with black and fringed with smoke.
Get up, march off in direction of kitchen. Behind me knife is again banged against vodka glass. Reach dining-room exit just as non-linguist

waiter comes charging in. He's getting wise, already carries tray containing: Two portions of ham, two huge glasses of vodka, two gigantic glasses of beer. Behind a curtain near dining-room exit sits "kolega". What is he doing? Drinking vodka and beer!
Feel like a small child, ordering such mild things as I want. Should perhaps also order vodka and beer. Might improve frame of mind. Return to my table. Officers now have fire-red eyes. But third order of ham, vodka and beer has already been consumed. Fourth is coming. Notice that while gulping fourth vodka, mustachioed brave pours most of liquor into his lip decoration. Doesn't bother him. His aim improves when following up with beer. Most of ham, however, is pushed into his uniformed tunic. Bon appetit mon vieux!
Now the two of them pay and get up. Doubt if they are destined to perform brave deeds in defense of Peoples' Democracy today. Eight o'clock is a little early for their condition.
Fortunately breakfast and Charles arrive simultaniously. Was just about to cheer myself up with vodka and beer.

Since the autumn of 1956, Breslau has changed more than the Hotel "Monopol". Construction is going on although, compared to the immense damage the city suffered, it is still not very much. A number of new buildings have been put up south of a street once called "Stadtgraben", along the former "Neue Schweidnitzer" and "Tauentzien" streets. A square formerly known as "Tauentzien-Platz" where everything was destroyed, is now almost completely fringed by new blocks of flats and office buildings.

Construction has also been begun in the center of the city and although most houses are still surrounded by schaffolding, this is certainly a considerable advance over the previous year. There are new buildings along the former "Schweidnitzer Strasse" south of the "Ring" (the latter is a street surrounding Breslau's famous City Hall), the "Schuh-brücke", which runs parallel to the "Schweidnitzer Strasse" and along two streets running at right angles to the former, the "Albrecht-" and the "Ohlauer Strasse". On the "Ring" itself many old buildings are being renovated, particularly on the two sides once known as "Nasch-marktseite" and "Sieben-Kurfürsten-Seite". The St. Elizabeth Church is intact and the City Hall itself shows no signs of damage.

In other parts of the town conditions are worse. Not far from the center there was a square called the "Neumarkt"—all houses around it have completely disappeared and the square is a dusty vacant lot. Further north around a church once named "Sandkirche" there are countless ruins. The cathedral, located nearby, has been partially repaired, but the top half of both its towers is still missing. The "Dom" street, which led from the cathedral to the "Sandkirche" has been completely repaired; with the aid of our old photographs and maps it was interesting to discover that the street and the buildings on both sides have been rebuilt in a slightly changed location, eliminating a curve in the street. The suburbs, called "Vorstädte" are for the most part still as shattered as they were at the end of the war. The "Niko-lai" and "Ohlauer" districts have hardly seen any reconstruction, while the "Schweidnitzer Vorstadt" is, as far as we could tell, the most severely hit and least rebuilt part of Breslau. On the main street leading south through this district, a street which is the exit from Breslau towards the Autobahn, one passes through a large area where not a single building is standing and the remains of houses have become overgrown by bushes and grass. Then, nearer the Autobahn, there is a Soviet cemetary, with a huge memorial decorated by the usual tanks and guns mounted on stone pedestals.

North of the river Oder, in the suburb once called the "Oder-Vorstadt" many gaps yawn in the rows of houses, and despite some newly built blocks of flats there are bombed out lots which stretch across many streets.

Hence Breslau still gives the overall impression of being a very serious-ly damaged city and since the rebuilding progresses slowly and for the most part is done with primitive means, it is likely that the situation will not alter appreciably for sometime to come. Last year we came to Breslau from Warsaw and Poznan and the condition we found here disturbed us deeply. Today we have learned to look at all this with much greater calm. We think that this is in part due to the first signs of reconstruction, and in part because we have become case-hardened. After Marienburg, Elbing, Kolberg, Pyritz and Küstrin, Breslau looks almost untouched.

Many of the large blocks of flats in which people are already living, are not really completed; they lack any outer finish; instead of main entrances they have wooden temporary doors and sometimes temporary window frames. We had seen some of these buildings in the same condition last year and have now noticed that no further work has been done on them. The month and year of construction is often chiselled in stone blocks over the entrances and so one can see that several reached the semi-finished stage in the autumn and winter of 1955 and still have not been completed.

Standing in front of one unfinished block we fell into conversation with a man who seemed to have something to do with the construction programme. I had already seen him at another building site where he was making an inspection.

I asked him point-blank why the buildings were not being completed and he told me that there was a grave shortage of sand and cement in all parts of Poland. It had therefore been decided that it was better to build many houses and not to finish them completely, than to construct a few perfectly. When I asked if this procedure did not affect the durability of the houses on the one hand and the health of the tenants on the other, the man was reluctant to commit himself. He merely said:

"When one has tens of thousands of people for whom one must provide a roof over their heads one cannot enter into long debates. One has to build as best one can."

Later I discovered a vegetable market which was also a sales center for all manner of used goods. It was located on the site of the former "Neumarkt" square in the midst of a field of rubble. Some temporary huts and stalls have been put up there and a number of private peasants also sell their products directly from their carts. The new policy initiated by the Gomulka administration, which calls for a reduction and eventual discontinuation of forced delivery quotas, already appears to have had a notable effect here. The market itself looked extremely shabby but I saw more and better fruits and vegetables on sale there than anywhere else in Poland.

We had already been told in Warsaw that the opportunity to leave collectives and state farms, which is being given to the peasants, was expected to result in further improvements in the general food supply. It was said that the grave shortage of foodstuffs which has existed in Poland for years would come to an end; however another hurdle would have to be overcome before this could happen: as already mentioned, the first indication that the peasants were tasting and exercising their new-found freedom was that they were hoarding their produce, hoping to force higher prices. But is is clear that this will not go on indefinitely, that farm produce which cannot be stored a long time, particularly vegetables and fresh fruits, will have to be brought to market. The marketing of meat cannot be stopped either for there is a severe shortage of feed-grain, which may indeed lead to forced slaughtering and a glut on the market. In any event the peasants surely do not plan to stop production of all food for a long period of time. They merely hope to use the means now at their disposal to make up for losses incurred over many years. Thus, even with such problems as hoarding still to be overcome, it may well be that the new Gomulka administration farm policy will soon bring tangible improvements for the entire country.

Near the market I found another aspect of private enterprise, although this was hardly a cheerful discovery: ten or twelve disabled war veterans had moved their wheel-chairs against the wall of a building and spread light bulbs, razor-blades, pencils and shoe-laces on their laps, which they were offering to passers-by with loud shouts and animated gestures. They were extremely friendly and insisted that I photograph them. While I did so, they joked among themselves and I repeatedly heard the word "reklama".—They had understood the meaning of free enterprise even to the need for advertising.

Jacqueline had remained in the car while I looked at the market and when I returned I was reminded of Heilsberg in East Prussia. Someone was leaning up to the waist into the car. This time it was no gipsy woman but a young lad who would not budge when I asked him to make room for me. A couple of explicit slaps on his backside did not move him either and I had to take him by his coat and trousers and pull him out of the window. He was completely drunk. I learned that he had told Jacqueline in a few mumbled German words that it was absolutely essential that he drive with us. When she had tried to chase him away he had declared:
"No, I stay here!" Then he had asked: "Where you live? In 'Monopol'?"
It was not hard to guess where we lived. The "Monopol" is the only "Orbis"-hotel in Breslau. But nonetheless Jacqueline was frightened and we hope that the drunken youth will not follow us to the hotel. Actually I suspect he is already sleeping it off somewhere in a corner. Outside the hotel and other large buildings we have seen an astonishing poster: it announces an evening of "Rock-'n'-Roll-dancing, featuring the appearance of a West-Indian calypso orchestra and a variety troupe with the marvelous name: "The Tremble Kids". This great cultural event is to take place after our departure from Breslau. A pity—one really should not miss such a thing.

The next day.—We did not miss the "Rock-'n'-Roll"! We had our own show all night long! However it was "Rock-'n'-Roll", Wroclaw version.
The wild to-do began shortly after we had gone to bed and fallen asleep. Our bathroom is separated from the adjoining one by a thin wall which stops a good three feet below the ceiling. The door to our bathroom was closed, but our neighbours had evidently left theirs' open and hence a perfect megaphone for the transmission of a special type of "Rock-'n'-Roll" was set up.
It all started with a boisterous rendition of the "Volga Boatman" roared by what I judged to be half a dozen men with fine vocal chords

and an unusual gift for atonal singing. Equally modernistic renditions of "Ole Man River", the Marseillaise, a Polish Folk Song and "Roll Out The Barrel" followed without intermission.

Although we were furious, we found the first part of this "programme" amusing enough to think of the "Rock-'n'-Roll" posters, to grin and bear it. There was no lack of rocking,—evidently plenty of it in front of the eyes of the vocalists, and more in our room, where glasses tinkled and cupboard doors opened.

Then speeches were being delivered next door, in a tone of voice loud enough to be heard in a large sports arena without a public-address system. It was not easy to understand what was being said, partly because several speakers suffered from extreme attacks of the hiccoughs and partly because the orators were constantly interrupted by cheers, laughter and table banging. I was able to establish that the speeches were both in Polish and in English.

"Those are the 'Tremble Kids'", Jacqueline said. She was right—there was no shortage of trembling.

Fortunately the West-Indian calypso orchestra didn't turn up, but we were not to be spared the "roll" part of the show. We couldn't quite understand what was happening, but something or somebody was being rolled about in the next room, accompanied by roars of laughter and more singing. Moreover, the internationally minded gentlemen next door were no longer satisfied to sing one song from far-off lands at a time; they now tried two together. Simultaneously rendered versions of the two river songs, "Ole Man River" and the "Volga Boatman" turned out to be a fascinating blend of dissonance. The other songs in their repertoire also sounded quite fantastic.

At half past four we had had more than enough. After I had tried in vain to bring the concert to an end by knocking on the wall, I put on slippers and dressing gown and went to see the night-porter. Since his desk is cunningly removed as far as possible from the switchboard, it hadn't been possible to reach him by telephone.

I found that faint-hearted moth in a state of near-hysteria.

"Yes, yes, I know," he twittered as soon as he saw me, "they are terrible, these people, terrible! but what should I do? they are Americans!"

"Americans? what in heaven's name are they doing here?" I inquired incredulously.

"I have no idea, no idea," the man moaned. "Whatever it is, I wish they would do it somewhere else!"

"And you can't go up there and tell them to stop making so much noise?"

"Please! imagine! they are eight men and they are big and fat and they have ordered six bottles of vodka! what should I say to them?" the porter whined and seemed ready to run away that very instant. I returned to our room. At six in the morning the "Rock-'n'-Roll" began to die down, and I heard some of the men saying something in English about going out for a walk.

"There'll be some rocking and some rolling when they reach the street," Jacqueline mumbled and at last we fell asleep again.

This morning one of the day-porters explained that an entire bus-load of Americans of Polish extraction had arrived in Breslau the previous evening. It had been the first night in twenty or more years that these men had spent on Polish soil, and this had naturally led to what the porter called "a little celebration".

The group is supposed to continue to Warsaw today, will then spend a few days in the capital before separating to visit relatives in different parts of the country.

Other groups in busses have also arrived here. Five coaches from West Germany are presently parked in front of the hotel. Last night they brought about 150 Germans for whom a tour of the former german territories has been organized. We were told that such groups pass through at regular intervals during the summer season. The people arrive late at night, have to wait around endlessly until they are assigned a room, then receive a coupon with which they must go and wait some more until a meagre dinner is served to them and early the next morning they continue on their way. One cannot say

233

that they see much of Breslau.—At the moment three Germans are standing in front of the hotel, talking to some people who—one can tell by their clothes—live here; perhaps they are relatives, perhaps friends, but certainly they knew each other well. After witnessing a touching reunion we moved away, hoping they would be granted at least a few minutes of privacy.

I wandered about through the over-filled hotel lobby, which seems almost international today, thanks to the English- and German-speaking travelers. Soon I landed back at the desk and asked the porter what he could tell me about the German visitors.

"They drive around," he said shrugging his shoulders. "They drive around and look at things."

One of the Germans heard this reply and asked me.

"Are you here on your own?" he showed amazement when I told him this was so. "Well, in that case you'll be able to see a lot more than we," he said. "But still, we tell ourselves,—a little is better than nothing at all."

I asked him whether his group consisted of Silesians.

"Yes, partly," he said, "but most of us are simply people like me,— either they are curious or they had or still have relatives here. Most native Silisians in the Federal Republic are glad that the're out and don't want to come back, while things are like this."

I asked the man whether he and his traveling companions had already gained any definite impressions.

"Well, yes, lots of impressions," he said, "but they're not very nice. Of course, one can't say very much, when one has just driven down the Autobahn and reached Breslau after dark. But one thing is sure, as far as I am concerned, anyway: Germany would be silly to take back Silesia the way it is now. It would be a millstone around our necks."

Just then another German traveler came to join us. He had evidently heard the other man's last remarks.

"Extraordinary declarations you are making there," he said angrily. "You are simply giving Silesia away, are you? I'll tell you, it's of no concern how this country looks at the moment. The only thing of any importance is that this was always german territory, and will always remain german territory. Once it's returned to us, then wait and see, we'll put it on its feet again in no time! We managed it out west, we'll manage it here!"

The first man wanted to say something in reply and several other Germans had meanwhile gathered around us, ready for what promised to become a heated argument. But chance—or design—would have it that just then the man from "Orbis" who was organizing the Germans' tour, announced the departure of the busses.

If the two men happened to be traveling in the same bus, then, I told myself, the discussion would surely be continued, for there was much to be said on this subject.

Meanwhile Jacqueline has seen to our supplies. The "kitchen" is already in the car. We are off towards the south-west, to Lower Silesia.

"I WILL REMAIN UNTIL THE LAST SERVICE"

Schweidnitz.—In what is now Swidnica there lives a man who can certainly be called the most notable German in these territories.

Pastor Herbert Rutz is one of the two last German protestant clergymen who are still in office here and attend to the religious and spiritual needs of the ever-shrinking German parishes. We are fortunate to have spent some interesting and in part moving hours with pastor Rutz, his wife and his daughter.

While we were still on our way to Schweidnitz we already felt sure that an unusual experience lay ahead. We considered it somehow significant that the purely practical obstacles which frequently have to be overcome during a journey in these regions were this time surmounted with astonishing ease.

As we left Breslau and found the sparingly marked road to Schweidnitz something happened that had occured many time before: what shields we could find suddenly contained no further reference to

Swidnica but only listed places which were not even to be found on our maps. We stood helplessly before one set of signs trying to decide which way our instincts would have us go, when a Polish car pulled up beside us and four men asked politely where we were heading.

"We're also going to Swidnica", said the driver when we had named our objective, "just drive behind us".

In this way we were soon in the outskirts of Schweidnitz. Our guides stopped and waved to us before continuing on their way.

We found the town to be partially destroyed and, as usual, greatly neglected but in an infinitely better condition than many communities in Pomerania and East Brandenburg.

We had heard a little about pastor Rutz before beginning this trip, knew that he lived in Schweidnitz, was considered to be an extremely brave man and that he carried on his work under very difficult circumstances. It seemed safe to assume that it would not be too hard to find someone who might tell us where the pastor could be located. Any protestant, certainly almost any German would surely be able to help us. For a while we drove slowly through the streets of the town until I spotted a man whose appearance led me to conclude that he was German. Again the difficulties were overcome with remarkable ease. The man was indeed a German, knew pastor Rutz, and told us how to get to him. However he took it for granted that I knew the town and apparently without thinking, called streets by names which no longer exist. I did not notice this either until we tried to follow his directions and failed. But the man had said that the clergyman lived "next door to the church" and so I decided not to bother anyone else and to continue on our way.

We could make out a high church steeple,—I have since discovered that it is the highest in Silesia,—and drove to it. This was not easy because many streets were blocked by rubble, others were torn up or designated as one-way streets despite the absence of traffic. Navigating busily, we did not ascertain whether the church was protestant or catholic, and when we had reached it, were so eager to meet pastor Rutz that we never thought to investigate further. All the doors of the surrounding buildings were locked. Only the church itself was open. I entered and saw two women with white kerchiefs on their heads, who were sweeping between the pew. I approached one and asked if she could speak German. She shook her head but indicated that her "kolega" could.

"Of course, I can speak German," the other woman said when I addressed her. "I am German."

When I asked where I might find pastor Rutz she smiled and explained that this was the catholic church.

"I am protestant myself, I only work here," she said, almost as if wishing to excuse her presence in a church of another denomination. As she continued to talk I only half listened, thinking that even here, under the present political system, in this twilight for christianity, the countless sectarian differences which make the so-called "free world" such an easy prey to totalitarianism, could not be laid to rest. The woman was saying something about the route to pastor Rutz's house, that it was difficult but that I would surely find it.

I had not paid sufficient attention. Could she possibly come with us and show us the way, I asked; I would be glad to drive her back to her work afterwards. She spoke in broken Polish to the other woman, nodded to me and we left the church. Again everything had been solved easily.

On the way to the car she asked me how we had come here. My explanation caused immense amazement. She shook her head and repeated several times:

"God is everywhere!"

She was very poorly dressed,—an ancient smock, torn wool stockings and shoes which were urgently in need of repair. She did not want to enter the car, declaring that she was not properly dressed to go for a drive. At length I persuaded her that it did not matter and we drove on. As we crossed the town she told us that she came from Breslau and had fled to Schweidnitz at the end of the war because the Germans were not being persecuted as vehemently in the smaller towns.

"I am a member of the German Club here," she said. "We have our club again and we're allowed to speak German in public. Not long ago it could happen that you were beaten if they heard you speaking German. It was terrible. I have been in prison twice already. Both times because I was falsely denounced. Somebody went to the police and complained about me. I don't know who and I don't know why. I was simply put in jail.

"But now we have our club again, and of course our church," she went on, "and that helps us a lot. The club is becoming smaller and smaller, because people are able to leave now, and so they move away as quickly as they can."

I asked if she had relatives in Germany who would enable her to leave too.

"Oh yes, I have people," she replied, "but I have become old, and I have trouble deciding whether it is worth going away from here."

"But wouldn't it be better for you to emigrate,—I mean economically?" I asked.

"Oh yes, I suppose. But, you see, somehow I still hope that one of these days Silesia will become German again."

She was sitting behind me. Suddenly she leaned forward and asked urgently:

"Don't you think that it is possible?"

I replied that I did not consider a return of these territories to Germany likely at this time. She sank back into the seat and sighed.

"All the young people say that,—and that is why they are leaving," she murmured.

I asked: "I have been told that life in general has become easier here. Is that right?"

"Oh well, yes, it is a little better," the woman said after a pause. "It isn't quite so terrible any more. As I said, we Germans have been granted a few more rights and we can—how shall I say?—move a little more freely. And it's possible to buy more goods,—that sort of thing. But you know, there is something to which we Germans can never become accustomed: we are used to neatness, orderliness, to have everything proper, and the Poles do not think that way at all,—not the way we like to have things in order. And the drunkenness! You are in danger of your life if you go out into the street at night. That is the worst of it: the lack of proper order—no discipline."

We had come to an attractive small park, with high trees, and surrounded by a garden wall. We left the car before a locked iron gate and entered through a side door. In the park, almost hidden by the trees, stood a large old church. It seemed to be entirely of wood. Nearby there were several brick buildings.

"This property once belonged to our parish," our guide told us. "The church, these living quarters, everything. I don't know who owns what today." She pointed out one of the brick buildings. "This is where pastor Rutz lives—upstairs." Then we drove her back to the catholic church.

On the return journey the woman confessed that she did not like pastor Rutz.

"I don't know exactly where he comes from, and I don't know how it is that he manages to get along with the authorities. Somehow I have a feeling he is politically ... I don't know,—I cannot express it properly."

This made me more eager than ever to meet the clergyman and hear what he could tell us about his life and work.

Then again there was the apology,—or perhaps I only imagined it? "I only work in the catholic church as a cleaning woman because there are so few opportunities to earn something. For a woman of my age it is not easy. I also work as a seamstress, but that doesn't bring me much money." And then she added with a sigh: "I was a teacher in a technical school, it is quite a change for me. For thirteen years I served The Reich with great joy!"

There was a sound to the way she spoke the words "Reich" and "joy" which I did not like,—once more it could be mere coincidence, or a combination of words evoking a memory which is best forgotten. We thanked the woman for her help and she returned to her work. "God is everywhere," she said on leaving us.

Pastor Rutz was at home. Frau Rutz was washing the laundry when we arrived and she led us into the combined dining-room-living-room-study of the tiny flat. The pastor sat at a long table, working an a sermon.

The following are the notes I made during the hours we spent with this extraordinary man:

Herbert Rutz is a native of Silesia, a man of some fifty years, with grey hair and a grey mustache. He wears horn-rimmed spectacles. As if the circumstances under which he must perform his duties were not complicated enough, he suffers from a severe physical handicap: his left foot is so crippled as to be practically useless. We notice this as he rises to greet us. He is only wearing one shoe and moves with great difficulty, using two crutches.

We introduce ourselves to him and explain the purpose of our visit. Soon we are sitting at the long table and the pastor excuses himself for not having met us in the hall. "Just now I am having a lot of trouble with my foot," he says.

He explains that his foot was seriously injured a few years ago; too much physical strain and a lack of the right medicaments had worsened the injury so much that something which the pastor thinks might be tuberculosis of the bone has set in.

Frau Rutz, who has now joined us, explains a little more:

"He cannot be persuaded to rest even a little bit. At least here at home, he takes off the shoe, and when he only goes over to the church, he uses the two crutches. But when he is going a little further away, —and that is almost all the time—then he believes that it is not good if he attracts too much attention and looks as if he were a sick man. And so he only uses a prosthesis and a walking stick. And that makes his foot worse and worse."

"But you see," the pastor himself adds, "the world around me is so severely encumbered—I mean metaphorically speaking—that it would not be right for me, of all people, to make a show of being physically encumbered."

After a few questions the story of this injury is told: due to a previous accident, the foot was already sick at the end of the war. Then the pastor and his family had to flee from his upper silesian parish. As soon as people could return to the parish again, the pastor decided to go back too. He was walking along the war-torn roads of Silesia, when a Russian tank knocked him down causing serious injury to his bad foot. Meanwhile the wound has become incurable.

This does not prevent him from doing his duties, day in and day out. He cares for a community of two thousand German protestants.

It is not just one parish. In fact it is an area made up of nineteen congregations which have lost their pastors long ago. Breslau belongs to these—there being only a few German protestants left in the city— and Jauer, a lower Silesian town where there is still a concentration of about nine hundred Germans. Then again the area comprises places like Bad Altheide, where only fourteen parishioners remain.

Pastor Rutz visits these nineteen places regularly, conducts services there, supervises the pre-confirmation instruction and concerns himself with the countless spiritual needs of this far-flung community. He has five lectors who help him as much as they can, but the bulk of the work must be and is done by the pastor himself.

The story of his life, since his accident, reads like an adventure story: due to his enjury he was virtually unable to work during five years. Frau Rutz earned a little money by knitting for the Russian occupation forces. Then the pastor learned the shoemaker's trade, and managed to make some money in this way. Later there was a serious shortage of book-keepers in the entire East, and since he knew a little about accountancy, the pastor was hired by a Polish concern. In 1951 he learned that a pastor was urgently needed in the district of Schweidnitz. But the parish was very poor and the pressure on the German population great, hence a full-time vicar was not even thought of. Pastor Rutz had a solution: he took a night train every Saturday and traveled from Upper Silesia to Schweidnitz, arriving in the morning; there he conducted the services, then took the train back. In 1952 he was able to move permanently to Schweidnitz. But the parish was still too poor to support him and he got himself a job as a book-keeper in a state concern in the town. In 1954 the parishioners were able to find the means to pay him some money, so that he was able to devote himself to this real work full-time. Since then he has worked here virtually day and night.

Pastor Rutz owns no means of transportation. Because of his foot he cannot even use a bicycle. Hence he depends on the railway and busses; but since these provide infrequent service, he often requires half a day to visit a part of his parish which is a mere twelve miles away. Sometimes he tries to hitch-hike, but since there is so little road traffic, this is an unreliable way of moving about.

Eveline, the pastor's thirteen year old daughter, currently attends the German school in Schweidnitz. But there are only six classes in this school, and as the girl has reached the senior class, there will be no further opportunity for her to receive tuition in her native tongue. Therefore she is now learning to play the organ, so that she will be able to become organist in her father's church. Some time ago there were six parisioners in Schweidnitz who could play the organ well enough for church services; now all but one have emigrated. Eveline will be a welcome replacement.

The parish shrinks from day to day. The two thousand members are what is left of six thousand five hundred who were here when the pastor moved to Schweidnitz.

And this is what pastor Rutz has to say about his arduous work and his parish:

About the life of the Germans:

"In the past everything was done to make the people's life as difficult as possible. Even today they are still treated roughly, but there are improvements. Occasionally the school children throw stones at my daughter, but she is used to that.

"The Germans who are left here stick together as best they can. Germans marry Germans and bring me their children for baptism."

About religious services:

"We are permitted to hold services, but there are plenty of difficulties just the same. The Lutheran Church has been placed under the Polish Protestant Church. Whatever our parish owned now belongs to the Polish church. Before I came here, our parish was permitted to conduct services only in the baptismal chapel. The official reason was, that there was only a lector here who was not really qualified to conduct services in the church itself.

"In Breslau a completely polonized German is the chairman of the church council. My parishioners there are not permitted to use their own church for their services and must use a totally inadequate room. For confirmation the members of the parish must travel an hour and a half by train to the next church.

"I myself cannot have any contact with the church to which I really belong: the Evangelical Church in Germany. I am my own superior, my own subordinate, and also my own sexton."

About religious instruction in the schools:

"Since Gomulka religious instruction in the schools has been permitted again. Before that we gave instruction here, in our house. My wife did most of the teaching while I was still working as a book-keeper."

About the regulations which he, as pastor, must observe:

"I am only permitted to look after German parishioners. It is not always easy to decide who is a German and who is not; there are many people who were Germans by birth and language and now have Polish documents—either by choice or because they were required to have them. There was a time during which one could chose. When the identity cards were issued in 1951, one could not acquire Polish citizenship directly, but could declare oneself to belong to the Polish people's community. Incidentally I did not do this, and I will tell you why: shoddy principles are no principles. I am not a Pole. My wife cannot even speak the language. I cannot go to the pulpit, carrying a lie. But of course, this makes my life and my work that much harder."

About the emigration of the Germans:
"Now that it is easier to receive travel papers, the people leave as
quickly as they can, because they fear that the frontiers will be closed
again. And they are right to go, for there is no future for them here,
particularly for the young ones. By the way, people are wrong who say
that only those can go who have relatives in Germany. As far as I
know, anyone having Polish documents has no trouble emigrating,
whether there are relatives abroad or not."

We are still sitting in the all-purpose room of this small apartment.
We are asked to lunch and accept only under the condition that we
may contribute our supplies, which we would have eaten anyway. It
is difficult to persuade Frau Rutz to accept this suggestion, but at
last we succeed.
Grace, spoken quietly by pastor Rutz, suddenly converts this room
in Polish Silesia into a place of warmth and intimacy.
During the meal I ask the question which has been on the tip of my
tongue throughout the previous talk with the clergyman: the parish
is emigrating, dying out as it were. What will become of the pastor
himself?
"Well, perhaps I will also move to West Germany," he replies, "but
not yet. There is still much work for me here. Of course, if I were
to apply for travel papers now, we could leave right away. The authorities would be quite pleased if I were to disappear. In their eyes I
contribute to keeping the remaining Germans together and that is
not wanted. But as I say there is still much to be done. I will remain
until the last service."
I ask pastor Rutz what his thoughts are while he carries on with
his difficult task.
"It must be! It is a duty which I have imposed on myself," he says.
"But sometimes I become rather sad and feel as if I were standing
in a cemetery. In a cemetery in which there are not even the gravestones which remind of the past. But one must not think about these
things too much. Work must come first."

This work continues today as everyday. In Reichenbach there is to be pre-confirmational instruction this afternoon. The bus is leaving shortly.

"I must get ready," pastor Rutz says. It is clear that he is primarily thinking of his injured foot. We tell him that he is not taking any bus today. We are driving him to Reichenbach.—There is not so much hurry now and the pastor can show me his church.

He walks through the garden with astonishing agility, past the trees to the beautiful church.

"In the middle ages, when this church was built, the local feudal lord required that not a single nail be used," the pastor relates with a smile. "He hoped that this would help to destroy the church in a short time. Today we discover that this church has survived better than many another." Soon his further thoughts find expression: "Now we are sharing the church with the Polish parish, and the day may come when none of us will be here to represent our share." And he points at a little stack of German hymn books lying on two chairs in the church. "There are not many of these left either. But I believe all this is of secondary importance. The church will continue to exist.

Jacqueline also has some notes about the Rutz family which belong to this story. They follow:

"Anyone who lives in the center of a country cannot imagine what it means to live in a frontier district." With this remark Frau Rutz begins to reminisce about a life in which difficulties, pressures from without, never ceased. The years before the war which the Rutz family spent in the upper Silesian frontier area were a sort of preparation for the things to follow in the postwar years:

"The word 'peace' never had any meaning for us," she says. "The arguments and crises between Germany and Poland, the charged atmosphere, always determined our life. Mercifully one accustoms oneselfs to many things in time. Otherwise life under these circumstances would be impossible."

Frau Rutz tells me this and other things while the pastor is showing Charles the church. I learn that the pastor and she have found a way of accepting the ever-present difficulties in their lives, but that the thirteen year old Eveline has understandably not been able to do this yet.

"She is not inured, in fact one could almost say she's orphaned. You see the child has practically no friends of her own age. The few German children who still live here are spread all over the area and mostly stay at home. During the years of the persecution of the Germans, all social life came to an end and has not been revived. We ourselves only see the other parishioners in connection with my husband's work. It is not possible to do it otherwise."

Frau Rutz tells of the serious problems which arise in connection with the education of her daughter:

"Of course we try to give the little one as much schooling as possible at home, in order to fill-in the gaps which developed at school. But even this is very difficult. Neither my husband nor I have very much time. We have hardly any German books, just the few which we were able to save from our previous house."

Eveline is friendly and cheerful but she looks pale and weak. I mention to Frau Rutz how little the girl ate at lunch.

"Yes, yes, all this is part of this form of being orphaned," Frau Rutz replies. "She does not get into the fresh air enough and I cannot expect of her to play alone all the time or to do something else for her health without company. So she remains pale and does not have enough appetite. We are always wracking our brains what we could do. We even thought of the Polish children's holiday camps of which there are several. But the children return full of lice and other vermins and so we cannot bring ourselves to send Eveline. It is a blessing that she is such an even-tempered child. But still I fear for her future. When we will go to West Germany what will happen to her? She will never be able to fit anywhere and will always be a lost soul. My husband and I, we are—as I said—used to it, hardened, and when we will go to the West we will surely find the strength to

make our way. But with a child of this age it is so very difficult.
This is our biggest problem. You see, we are living in a vacuum."

Here end the notes of our conversations with the Rutz family in
their home.

When the clergyman and I returned from the church, we said good bye
to Frau Rutz and her daughter and drove the pastor to the near-by
town of Reichenbach in the Eulen Mountains.

We were a little behind schedule. "If only the children haven't gone
home," the pastor said, anxiously looking at his watch. "When I
began this confirmation class I had eighteen children. Now there are
four. The others have all emigrated. And I do not want to have the
four leave the class while they are still here. One has to do everything possible to give these young people moral strength."

As we approached Reichenbach, which now has the name Dzierzo-
niow, the pastor told us that there are many Jewish repatriates in the
town, who had only recently returned from Russia. I asked whether
besides anti-German feelings, the other Polish inhabitants of the town
were also showing anti-semitic tendencies.

"It could very well be," the pastor replied, "but it is important to
keep away from these incitements to hate whenever possible."

We stopped before a rather large protestant church and the pastor
led the way to the vestry. He was clearly relieved to find that the
four pupils were still there. The elder of the local church was also
on hand and greeted us warmly.

The vestry was a tiny room, lit feebly by a single bulb suspended
from the high ceiling. The pupils,—two girls and two boys,—
answered the pastor's first questions while I took photographs in
order to complete my sequence of pictures showing the clergyman's
work, which I had begun earlier. Soon I was certain that he had had
enough of us, our endless queries and the repeated flashes of the
photographic equipment. But as he had done from the beginning, he
endured all this with great calm and dignity and when we finally

bade him farewell, he gave our journey his blessing and wished us a safe return home.

Now we have stopped outside Reichenbach,—a town in which hardly any war-time damage was to be found,—to correlate our many notes and impressions and to prepare for the next leg of our trip.

We are heading for the Western tip of Lower Silesia.

ADDENDUM

The notes concerning pastor Herbert Rutz have had to be extended. After we had left the German territories under Polish administration, we received a card from Schweidnitz, which read:

> "On August the 22nd 1957, my
> beloved husband, our good
> father and son,
>
> PASTOR HERBERT RUTZ
> died suddenly and unexpectedly.
> Funeral services were held on
> August the 26th, at the Peace
> Church, interment was at the
> protestant cemetary, Swidnica,
> Plac Pokoju."

This news was a great shock. We knew how sick pastor Rutz was, but he was so active, had so much mental and physical vitality, that it is hard to believe his life on earth has ended. Needless to say, his death is a great loss to his family—and this really includes the two thousand people in nineteen parishes, to whose spiritual needs he attended. But it is also a profound loss for many people outside his direct sphere of activity: for all those who are convinced that the future of this world must not depend on power politicians and the inventors of more fearful machines for destruction, but rather on those who are unshakable in their faith, their determination to do their duty and serve their fellow-men. Herbert Rutz was such a man. He is no longer. We all grieve at his passing.

"WHAT'S THAT, KAMIENKA GORA?"

En route to Hirschberg.—First we drove back to Schweidnitz, then turned north-west and drove to Freiburg-in-Schlesien.

Half-way between Schweidnitz and Freiburg we passed a little village, which does not appear on our German map, but bears the Polish name Mokrzeszow. There we saw one notable building which may have been a monastery; though outwardly undamaged, its inside was totally burned out. We were reminded of that part of Austria, which before 1955 was occupied by the Russians; in that area one can see numerous church buildings in a similar condition; perhaps the one in Mokrzeszow is also a memento left by the Red Army.

Freiburg (Swiebodzice).—The records say this was once an industrial town with 10,000 inhabitants. Some factories are in operation, but the population is certainly much reduced. The city looked empty, although war-damage was not considerable.

In order to see more of the southern part of Lower Silesia, we made a left turn at Freiburg and headed south. Barely 200 yards after the turn we saw a sign which we had seen in Danzig at every other street-corner: "Objazd". Our dictionary translates this as meaning "circular tour"—but we know better by now, it means: road torn up, take a side road. It also means—you're lucky if you get back to the main road somewhere along the way.

In this case the side-trip turned out to be worth while. The road we had to take led us into an enormous park and then through a splendid gate with fine wrought-iron filigree and an elaborate coat of arms connecting two massive stone pillars.

We stopped. There was no sign of a villa or chateau. Suddenly a grey car, a czech-made Skoda, came speeding up behind us and halted, breaks squealing. A man leaped out and ran to us.

"Where are you going?" he demanded in a somewhat unpleasant tone, speaking German with an accent. There is nothing about us or our car which suggests that we speak German, yet, as had happened frequently before, this Pole automatically switched to German when faced with a foreigner.

"Do you know the name of this park?" I enquired, trying to sound friendly and ignoring his question.

"You are perhaps going to Waldenburg? or to Hirschberg?" the man asked, evidently bursting with curiosity.

I pressed the accelerator and we sped away. I still react badly to inquisitions.

Jacqueline complained, saying that before Gomulka this man would almost certainly have been a policeman, but now he was probably nothing more than a man who considered us a sensation.

She was right. The Skoda followed us for a while, but in Waldenburg (where, to our amazement, we did get back to the main highway) he turned off and we did not see him again.

Waldenburg.—This town is now called Walbrzych, but despite the Polish name, it is said to be the main center of the German minority in Silesia.

Pastor Rutz had told us this and explained that the large protestant parish was being cared for by a clergyman who was of German origin but had polonized his name. It was therefore inevitable, the pastor had told me, that the entire Waldenburg parish followed the vicar's lead and became increasingly polonized. The woman who had taken us to the Rutz family had also said something about Waldenburg: the town had not suffered at all when the Russian armies had advanced into the area, she had declared, claiming that this had been made possible by the local German population which had embraced communism at just the right moment.

Waldenburg lies in the heart of the lower Silesian coal-mining district; it is possible that at the end of the war there were some communists among the coal miners, but we are more inclined to believe that the town excaped destruction because the coal mines were to be saved. As we looked around, we saw almost no signs of war-damage. The town was dirty, but not so much due to neglect as the everpresent coal dust and smoke from the nearby collieries.

Many people were in the streets and we saw several private cars with licenses beginning with the letter "H". We planned to drive on to Landeshut, the next town on our route, and asked a young man for directions. He turned out to be a Pole but spoke German. He not only explained the way, but also volunteered some information about himself.

"I am a mine worker," he said, adding proudly: "and I also own an automobile."

"I hear you are well paid," I said.

"Not bad," the young man replied. "Two thousand, three thousand a month. Some of us get to four thousand."

Compared to the average for Poland of about 1,000 Zloty a month, this was indeed quite a lot.

"So you are satisfied, are you?"

"Oh yes,—but of course, the work is hard."

He gave us a friendly smile as we drove on.

We soon found the road to Landeshut,—Kamienna Gora,—but before leaving Waldenburg wanted to try and talk to one more German in this German center. We looked around but no one was in sight. Evidently we had already driven too far out of town. Before us lay the huge pit-heaps, grey and bare, between which our route wound its way to Landeshut, fifteen miles further west.

At last we saw a man and immediately agreed that he had to be a German. The reason: his walk and his clothing. He was certainly past sixty, sternly erect, with a stiff military gait. He wore an old black peak cap, pulled down almost to his ears, a black three-quarter-lenght coat and a black scarf wound around his neck. And as if to complete his unmistakably turn-of-the-century middle-class German get-up, he also had a walking-cane and led an ancient, puffing, bandy-legged German Schnauzer by a leash.

I stopped beside him and greeted him in German.

"Tach!" was the reply. We had not heard this typically North-German bark of a greeting since our last visit to Berlin.

"Could you possibly tell me how to get to Kamienna Gora?" I asked, purposely using the Polish name for near-by Landeshut.

"What's that, Kamienna Gora?" the man barked at me.

"Landeshut," I explained.

"Oh, Landeshut! Well, just drive straight ahead here!"

The frosty way in which he had reacted to the Polish name was soon put aside and the man chatted amiably with us.

There were still many Germans here, he confirmed, but their number was decreasing rapidly, for the emigration movement was currently at its peak.

"They kept us here, because of the pits," the old man said. "They wouldn't have known how to work them. Now that we have taught some Poles, now we can go."

"Are you still in the mines?" I asked.

"No. I'm pensioned off. But that's nothing nice here."

"Do you plan to leave?"

"Yes, of course, as soon as it's arranged. The old lady down there," and he pointed at his dog, "the old lady and I, we'll get out of here as soon as we can. Eh, old one?"

The dog gasped as if in agreement, the old man raised his cane to his cap in greeting and we drove on.

The villages which we passed on our way to Landeshut, looked like miner's settlements anywhere. The war appeared to have passed them by and we thought that even many a former Silesian would find few profound changes here. It may be that everything is somewhat dirtier than before, but basically a coal mining area is always the same— West or East, capitalist or communist.

Landeshut is already outside the coal mining region. Hence: less dirt. But there was no corresponding increase in unrepaired war-scars— perhaps the textile concerns of the town were also to be spared.

Several factories were working, but we doubt whether the town has 14,000 inhabitants today, as it had had before the war.

We then followed a winding route, through forests and fields which led to the Schmiedeberger Pass. From the summit of the pass we saw the panorama of the Riesengebeirge, a mountain region which used to be among Germany's best known holiday centers. Below us, in the valley, nestled the little town of Schmiedeberg.—A short time later we reached the most important town in Lower Silesia, Hirschberg.

Hirschberg (Jelenia Gora).—Here is a town, which has suffered as much damage after the war as many another community did during the actual fighting.

According to former inhabitants who are now in the West, there was no fighting, no bombing in Hirschberg. The Russian armies advanced to Berlin further to the North and bombing the town did not seem worth their while. Yet, the famous baroque market square of Hirschberg looks as though a hand-to-hand battle had just taken place there. The gabled houses of the square are intact on two sides, but elsewhere, particularly in one corner, they have in part collapsed and in part are in advanced stages of desintegration. Some reconstruction work has been begun and supports have been put up to prevent one or two of the elaborately decorated walls from falling down. But there are many ruins.

While I stood on the roof of the car and took some photographs, the usual crowd gathered, which, in turn attrachted a militiaman. The officer pushed his way through to us, and finding not only foreigners but an attentive audience, decided to examine us thoroughly. I climbed down from the roof and had to submit documents for five minutes before he saluted and left. During the inspection, and even more so when he left, the policeman was greeted by cat-calls and remarks which, judging by their tone and by the general laughter of all present, were certainly not flattering. But the people smiled at us and ran after us delightedly when we moved fifty yards to take pictures from a different angle.

I had no sooner climbed back on the car's roof than another militia-man elbowed his way through the crowd. I explained that we had just been controlled, and the people, vehemently taking our side, talked to the man in Polish. This only strengthened his determination to see our "dokumenty". After the procedure was completed once again, the second policeman withdrew, accompanied by jeers and laughter. We rather wished the crowd would be a little less friendly towards us and thanked our lucky stars that one of the policemen did not try to show off by arresting us on some trifling pretext.

Until then we had not heard a single word of German. But as we were about to drive a little further a poorly dressed middle-aged woman came to Jacqueline's window, leaned well into the car and whispered in German:

"Oh, if you could only take me with you!"

She said that she hoped to be able to leave Hirschberg one of these days, but that she had applied for travel papers months ago and had heard nothing since then.

"And all the Poles here say to me: 'Why don't you go away? go on, get out!' and what shall I tell them? I am waiting and cannot leave!"

She shook our hands fervently, as if talking to us had helped her, and disappeared into the crowd.

In other parts of Hirschberg we again found a mixture of shattered, and unharmed but badly neglected buildings. There were no signs of reconstruction or even repair anywhere else in the town. Yet, on the market square a few baroque buildings were being restored at no doubt considerable cost—after they had been allowed to collapse. Our fable of the child and the toys came to mind again.

In the mountains.—The German dramatist Gerhart Hauptmann lived and died in Agnetendorf, a village in the mountains west of Hirsch-berg—the Riesengebirge. It was our intention to drive to Agnetendorf to visit the Hauptmann villa. Not as easy a project as it sounds. "Agnetendorf" does not exist any longer. When we had reached the foothills of the Riesengebirge and, passing through several villages, had asked some Poles about the village and the Gerhart-Hauptmann-villa, people shrugged their shoulders and looked blank.

There seemed to be no Germans in these villages. But as Hauptmann had died at a time when this area was already under Polish admini-stration, I still hoped that someone had heard of his name. One man —he looked like a farmer—appeared to know what we were seeking. He said we should drive back about two miles and then turn to the right and go up into the mountains.

He seemed quite sure of himself, yet we wondered if he really knew what we meant. We had had some bad experiences with directions given us by people on the roads. After some debate we decided not to follow the man's directions. Instead, we continued on the same main highway west from Hirschberg. After a few hundred years, Jacqueline exclaimed:

"There! ask this man! he's a German!"

One develops a "nose" for finding Germans in this country. The man whom Jacqueline had pointed out—he was perhaps fifty, had reddish-blond hair and wore plus-fours and a sports jacket—was indeed a German.

He told us that the way to Agnetendorf was not too difficut to find. Unfortunately he was expected at home after his walk from work, otherwise he would gladly have gone with us and show us the way. Then he hesitated for a moment and changed his mind.

"Oh, I think I can manage to make it alright," he said and smiled. "If you have room for me, I'll be glad to show you the way."

It turned out that the previous information had been correct; we drove back about two miles and then turned right, to a place called Jagniatkow. It almost sounded like Agnetendorf,—and it was.

Our guide spoke Polish fluently and, once we had reached the little mountain village, asked several people about the Hauptmann house. Here Polish people knew the villa by its late owner's name and it wasn't long before we had reached our objective. The villa stands on a wooded hill; it is in excellent condition, a large structure with one wing constructed in the shape of a tower, and big windows affording a fine view of the surrounding mountains. We mentioned to our companion that the house looked as if it had recently been renovated.

"That's right, it has," he said. "It is going to be used as a children's home."

Some of the children who were to spend their holidays there had already arrived. We heard their loud, cheerful voices from an upper storey of the house.

"I don't think this place will look so nice for long, once a whole army of children is let loose on it," I said.

"I am afraid you are right," our companion agreed. He had spoken very little until now and seemed reluctant to go into details on any subjects. On our way back into the lower valley we introduced ourselves and told him a little of our journey; now he appeared to be much relieved, and insisted that we come to his home "for a glass of wine". His manner changed completely. He had been polite before, but now he seemed delighted to have met us.

"I am afraid I haven't much to offer you," he said apologetically, "but I know we still have a little wine left, because last week was my birthday. It would be a fine late birthday present, if you would come."

On the way to his home the man told us that he used to be the owner of a large distillery and wine distributing firm in Upper Silesia. And once again a life story filled with odysean adventures unfolded before us: flight from Upper Silesia, leaving everything behind, years spent as a farm worker, as a construction hand, and at last the arrival here, in this outlying district of Silesia, as far away as possible from the big centers, where life was most difficult for a man of German origin. Here he worked as a book keeper in a state concern, earning a salary of 1,200 Zloty a month, an amount on which he, his wife and their two young children cannot live, but merely exist.

In their flat we met his wife. She was so over-worked and chronically nervous, that she could literally only drag herself about.

The apartment consisted of two wretched little rooms in a neglected former villa; yet it contained a few beautiful and in part valuable objects,—glassware, silver, a pair of candlesticks,—the silent witnesses of a life led under quite different circumstances.

Again we heard of countless difficulties, of the limitations, persecutions which had to be borne for years by so many people of German origin who did not manage to leave these territories in time. And again we heard of the hope, recently returned, that emigration would soon be possible.

The couple spoke of the "intellectual stultification" brought on by life under these circumstances,—of knowning one's books by heart since years, of not having been to the theater or a concert in fifteen years. We were told of hours spent every day after work, giving the children extra lessons, so that they would not begin life "mentally stunted", and of the feeling of utter frustration due to the lack of contact with the outside world.

"We hardly know what is going on anywhere outside these rooms," the man said. "Until quite recently it wasn't even possible to listen to foreign radio stations. You never knew if a secret policeman wasn't listening below your window."

We drank the wine left over from the birthday, and for a moment even the wife looked less nervous, less hunted.

"Perhaps we would not even think of emigrating, despite all the difficulties," the man went on. "But we must, because of the children. They cannot grow up here. Only Germans who are skilled labourers are comparatively well off. The Poles needed them, and they still need them today. For instances, there's the Josephinenhütte, the famous glass-works, near here; without German specialists, they would have had to close the place down. So the specialists were pampered!

"But for the general public there will not be a normal life here, as long as the Polish administration continues. In fact, I believe that the Poles themselves are not convinced they have been given these territories in perpetuity. And it is for this reason that they only do a minimum to keep things going and neglect land, buildings,—everything in fact. They speak of 'for ever and always' and calculate in terms of months and years."

We have now stopped on the highway between Hirschberg and Breslau and have noted our most recent experiences. Around us lies the land with the uncertain future. Dusk has fallen. The gloomy light corresponds with our mood.

"GREAT POLAND—LITTLE LAND FOR GREAT PEOPLE"

Liegnitz.—We left Breslau, our Silesian headquarters, very early this morning. First we drove some 40 miles west on the Autobahn and then turned off to Liegnitz. In this town, which is now called Legnica, are the headquarters of the Russian Warsaw Pact forces.

We passed the place where last year we had been turned back by soldiers because then,—perhaps temporarily—Liegnitz had been in a restricted zone. Now we again saw many soldiers, but certainly no more than in or around Sagan.

We drove to the old city hall and there photographed a famous exterior: the "Gabeljürge"-fountain, with some of the old buildings around it in the background. The houses are all standing in this street, but they have been neglected so long that the mortar is peeling off in large flakes. The people who gathered around us looked equally neglected. They were immensely dirty and although it was early morning several of them were drunk. In other parts of the town buildings have been damaged or torn down but quite a bit of new construction has gone up, much of it in a pseudo-modern and rather ugly style and done with such poor materials that parts of walls are beginning to crumble again. The two most important churches, the St. John's Church (Johannis-Kirche) and St. Peter's and St. Paul's (Peter- und Paul-Kirche) are intact. In front of the Johannis Kirche there was a public garden with well-kept flower beds—a rarity in this territory.

In the streets we met three police cars filled with militiamen and countless Russian military vehicles. The passengers in these cars were so obviously interested in us that we decided to drive on as soon as possible.

Lüben.—The whole "Ring", a circular street in the heart of what is now Lubin, is a shattered mass of stone and sand. Only a single building in the center was reconstructed and now serves as city hall. All the other old houses have vanished, save the church, which has a leaking roof and several damaged spots.

Some young lads watched me while I took photographs and looking at them, I felt sure they would fit perfectly into a street of an eastern Polish or Russian village. I photographed them too. They were delighted and shook me by the hand.

Outside Lüben, on the road leading north-west to Glogau, we stopped in front of a former German inn. The sad-looking building seemed to be a symbol:

"Gasthaus zum Hirschen," one could read over the entrance. The German writing was fading but still legible. Below it, a glass sign had been put up, baring the Polish word "Restauracja". The glass was already broken and looked almost shabbier than the original German writing on the wall.

As I took a photograph of the building, a Polish car—a new Russian model—came speeding up the street and stopped next to us. Two young men jumped out and asked the usual questions about our car,—price, horse-power, fuel consumption and so on. Then the driver of the car suggested that I sell him a few Dollars at the black market rate. When I refused, he said:

"I understand. Not here. Too public. We'll meet somewhere else."

I drove on and the other car followed. But the Pole did not understand that I merely wanted to be rid of him. Although I was soon well ahead, the road was too curvacious and uneven for me to get completely away from him. Once in a while I could still see him in my rear-view mirror. When we reached the village of Heerwegen, which is now called Polkowice, I quickly drove behind the parish church and stopped. A water pump was there. A man who spoke no language we could understand, but who kept on bowing to us in a touchingly polite way, ran to a near-by shop and brought us a drinking-cup. We were still drinking the clear cold water when the Polish car raced by on the other side of the church. Ten minutes later, after entering these notes in our diaries we were ready to go on.

Glogau (Glogow).—30,000 people once lived in this town! A castle was here, dating from the 17th century and a cathedral from the 13th and 15th centuries with a particularly famous baroque interior!— Herewith a tape-recording of my impressions of present-day Glogau:

I am walking through Glogau. Many feet of tape have run from one roll of the machine to the other without recording a single word; partly it's because I'm speechless,—speechless despite a journey of more than 3,600 miles through the ruins of what once was East Germany; partly because walking through the "streets" I have to be very careful not to fall.

To all intents and purposes Glogau no longer exists. Here a grotesque looking ruin, there a deep hole, then a hillock overgrown with sparce grass. Between all this I stumble about, microphone in hand, recorder over my shoulder. Over there, two goats. Four incredibly dirty children play around them. Nothing else is alive here.

On the very fringe of the former town there are a few houses. An old woman who was moved here from Poznan with her family told me out there, that not even ten per cent of Glogau survived the war and that almost nothing has been built here ever since. Three houses stand near the center of town: a cinema, a sort of cadet school and a former public building which is being used as a catholic emergency church, and is probably supposed to replace the shattered cathedral and all the other churches of Glogau.

Now I am standing on one of those hillocks made of rubble. As far as the eye can see there is nothing but devastation,—bits and pieces of buildings, a wall, a chimney, a tower, and then again rubble. The whole thing looks like an immensely enlarged picture of a horribly petrified vineyard, with twisted, gnarled vines held forever rigid, surrounded by grapes, withered and also petrified. One might call it horror-surrealism.

What was that? Music? No, singing! A marching song, sung by young voices. A marching song of the kind preferred by semi-military youth organizations. It sounds like an echo from the past. A past of which one certainly does not wish to be reminded; but memories are unavoidable, here in this petrified place,—memories of the beginning and the end of a dreadful period in history. A war, in which the world was to be conquered, and a terrible revenge met here, and in meeting left frightful traces. Before these traces have been wiped away by merciful time, youth is marching again, singing military songs!

A cold shudder runs down my spine.

End of tape.

Back to Breslau.—We drove back on a different highway, through Raudten, Steinau and Wohlau.

Seven miles after Glogau we passed a small village, now called Retka, which is not listed on our German map. We could find no one who spoke German and might have told us what the village was called before. After we had driven on, Jacqueline said:

"I would only put this sentence in my diary: we have just past through an incredibly dirty pig-sty."

Raudten, now Rudna, was not touched by the war, although it is hardly fifteen miles from here to Glogau. But the present inhabitants of Raudten slowly managed to make up for the damage the war did not do. The little town is desintegrating. One has the impression that it would almost be possible to watch while the houses collapse.

Shortly before Steinau we stopped at a state farm, recognizeable by the "P.G.R." sign over its entrance. The fields are in very bad condition. Many of them are fallow, while grain grows on others in feeble clumps. The buildings are all in a state of disrepair, the walls smeared with slogans, figures and drawings. Some of the workers, among them a woman and a small child, came out of the courtyard and were delighted when I photographed them. They looked Asiatic. In Steinau which is now called Scinawa, the bomb damage was once again immense. In the center of the town stood a huge Soviet war memorial, a black tank mounted on a stone pedestal. The square around the memorial was well kept. The rest of the town was grey and cheerless.

Wohlau (Wolow) shows just as much destruction. Even the parish church is destroyed. The only building in good condition was an enormous prison. At a level crossing a train rolled by, with cars on which huge signs announced that the passengers where repatriates. The train was going to Stettin. Perhaps these people will be used to fill up the empty spaces in Pomerania and East Brandenburg. Here, in western Silesia the population density is much greater. But the general collapse, the dirt, the economic crisis which is threatening everywhere, all this has developed just as far in this region as in the other former German areas under Polish administration.

The last tour.—Today we quit our headquarters in Breslau and drove first south and then east. We are planning to leave the former German territories today after visiting the upper Silesian coal-mining region. First we passed *Nimptsch* now renamed Niemcza. There we noticed a brewery which we had seen last year, while on the way from Poland to Czechoslovakia. Then it had been in operation, now it is idle. The town itself is extremely well-kept. We hardly saw a heap of rubble and not a single ruin.

Frankenstein (Zabkowice Slaskie) was also quite well-preserved. We stopped in the market square and I left the car to take some photographs. When I made my way back through the usual crowd, I found the following short note in Jacqueline's diary:

Waiting alone in car really no pleasure. Here in Frankenstein am again made aware of this. People around me everywhere. They press against car, press against me, leaning through windows, staring at everything inside, including me. This can lead to claustrophobia, also to fainting spells, if people leaning in smell as much of vodka as one man who was here just now. He came, pushed himself in front of my face, and nearly anesthetized me with his breath. Nine o'clock in morning, early for such anesthetic. He placed an enormous paw on my shoulder, turned correspondingly enormous face towards me.

"You from west," he declared in sort of basic German, using the familiar form of address, "Du" instead of the formal "Sie". Dramatic pause, then: "You from good place. You take me with you. I have relations in Cologne, Hannover. Nix good in Poland. Great Poland,— little land for great people. Me now going to work. Drunk. I know! But work is nix good. Life is nix beautiful. Nix is beautiful. So what I do? Drink!"

With that, great man from great Poland left me. His vodka-cloud is still floating in the car.—Don't know,—should one be shocked by such a man, find him repulsive? Or does he deserve pity? Anyway,— nix nice.

In *Kamenz*, now Kamieniec-Zabk, the castle which belonged to a branch of the German Kaiser's family is badly damaged. The castle is on a hill; below it, a church and a monastery are in much better condition. Oddly enough we met a Polish boy during our stop, who could speak a few words of German and even knew the original German name for the town.

In *Patschkkau* (Paczkow) the old city wall has collapsed. Before the war, our Baedecker informs us, it was completely preserved. We drove through the city gate at the northern end of the town but immediately had to come to a halt: the street was blocked by rubble.

263

"You cannot go on here, traffic is forbidden!" a man told me, first in Polish, then in fluent German. "This road is closed to all traffic. It is expected that many of the houses will fall down soon." It was easy to see that these expectations were justified.

We returned to the highway and drove east, past an artificial lake created for a hydro-electric development and on to Neisse.

Neisse is another one of those towns about which one must report that just about every famous building and monument—and there were many in what is now called Nysa—lies in ruins.

The "Schöne Brunnen", literally "the beautiful fountain", a world-famous piece of wrought-iron artistry from the 17th century, and once the landmark of Neisse, does not exist anymore. After a long search I found an iron pipe sticking out of the ground in a field of sand and stone, which, I finally concluded, was the water supply for the fountain. Near-by, I discovered a few pices of decorated stone-work which must have been part of the fountain's base.

The 290-foot high steeple of the city hall has gone.

The Jacobi-Church was severely hit, its separate bell-tower is nothing but a stump. A scaffold has been put around the nave of the church. Evidently some reconstruction is planned.

All the streets west of the Breslauer Strasse, the main street in which the "Schöne Brunnen" stood, are not to be found.

Only the famous "Kämmereigebäude", probably the finest example of late-renaissance architecture in Silesia, is being rebuilt. The basic structure has already been completed, but most of the elaborate decorations are still missing. So far the copy is perfect in every detail.

While I was photographing the "Kämmereigebäude", we went through another police control.

A blond young officer examined our papers. It was quite clear that he did not have the faintest notion what they meant and his embarassment was increased by the sarcastic grimaces and remarks made by an ever-increasing crowd around us. The mood of the people was far more hostile than it had been in Hirschberg; we were relieved when

264

the policeman, blushing and confused, returned our documents and left.

Five minutes later, while I was photographing the Jacobi-Church, we realized that this time the matter was not yet finished. The young militiaman had gone to fetch help. An enormous "kolega" on a motorcycle, with a civilian in the sidecar, came rushing up in a cloud of dust and in a very rude tone demanded to see all the documents we had. Our perpetual audience again displayed its deep-rooted hostility against this representative of the state. There can be no doubt that they woul never have dared this in the days before Gomulka.

It was not surprising that the policeman was annoyed by what was going on around him; but he, instead of retreating in confusion, showed his anger by taking more and more time over the examination of our papers. I am sure that his mood was not improved by the fact that two German women spoke to me in their native tongue and complained about their lives, while he was standing beside me.

I realized that the officer was doing his utmost to find some detail in our papers which was not in order, but having passed so many controls during the preceeding weeks, I felt reasonably sure he would not be successful. I was too optimistic. Having leafed through just about every paper, the policeman seemed to have found something after all: the rubber stamp on the first page of my International Driver's Licence had been put next to my photograph instead of covering one of its corners. This was wrong! I could sense how pleased the officer was. I showed him my Canadian and British licences but he would not be satisfied; it was improper that the photograph was not stamped. He would not change his mind about that. I thought: well, here we go! four thousand miles and four weeks of driving through this territory and no serious trouble with the militia. And now, on the last day, off we go, to jail, because a bit of rubber stamp was not pressed down where it should have been. My mind raced through all the possible ways one might avoid this: a bribe, a package of cigarettes, taking a picture of the man? No, he didn't look as if he would go for any of these. He was bent on proving his point. Taking the International Driver's License from him, I leafed through it, as if hoping to perform a magician's trick and make the stamp cover the photograph. Suddenly I noticed that on the last page of the booklet there was another stamp, although without a photograph. Simply because I could not think of anything else to do, I showed the last page to the officer. And without realizing it, I had performed the trick: apparently happy to have made his point, to have made me lose face before the crowd, he looked at the second stamp and nodded his head. That was alright, he said, but added a stern lecture about having the faulty photograph adjusted,—all this in a mixture of German and Polish in which his meaning, if not his every word, was amply clear. Then he remounted his motor-cycle and, dust swirling about him, departed as quickly as he had arrived.

We were relieved, feeling that this might well have been an ironical climax to our trip: a few nights spent in the jail at Neisse!

On the way to Oppeln we noticed many unusually neat fields and farms. Near *Falkenburg-in-Oberschlesien* (Niemodlin), we even passed a "P.G.R." farm which was well-kept and had new and freshly painted stables. In Falkenburg itself, not a single house was damaged on either side of the long market square and the 16th century castle was also in good condition.

Driving further east, farmers where harvesting fine crops of cherries from trees which lined both sides of the highway. Once again craving fresh fruit, we stopped and asked a man on a ladder if he would sell us some cherries. We had used our "pidgin" Polish. The farmer failed to understand. I tried again,—this time in German. The man laughed and answered,—he was a German. Yes, he would certainly sell us some fruit, he said and filled two of our plastic cups with ripe cherries.

"There are Germans all around here," he told us. "Between here and Oppeln and for quite a distance east of Oppeln, the villages are almost all a hundred per cent German. We were kept back here by the Russians and had to work on the state farms. Some of us, like myself, were then able to make ourselves independant again. Others are still working on the state farms."

When I asked whether there had been any improvement in general living conditions, the farmer said:

"Yes, things have improved. It still isn't wonderful but once can manage. Now my son has come back to me. He returned just recently from Russia. He was a prisoner-of-war. This way we can get by. Anyway, we do our best to lead a normal life."

We saw the manifestations of this "normal life" as we drove on: wherever we looked there were well-kept houses, freshly painted and surrounded by neat gardens. For the first time on our journey we saw flower-beds in private gardens. The fields were well looked after. The grain stood high and dense and "Potemkian Fields" were nowhere to be seen.

It was possible to draw a conclusion: people lived here who metaphorically and almost physically had roots in this soil. They were not strangers forced to live where they did not wish to be, longing for a home they had lost. They were people who were at home trying to live normal lives, even under difficulties. They were succeeding as most people succeed who are not uprooted, no matter what their nationality. That these were Upper Silesians and not Germans from other areas was worthy of note: they were people who had always lived close to Poland and the Polish tongue; many of them spoke the language, could get along with the new authorities and their representatives. In short, natural connections and roots had not been disturbed here and hence chaos had failed to progress.

In *Oppeln* (Opole) it was simple to find the center of town. The huge and not very attractive city hall in 19th century pseudo-italian style has been rebuilt, and its mighty tower, near the equally undamaged spire of the protestant church, can be seen from a long distance away. The patrician homes on the square around the city hall are all standing, giving the center of the town a pleasantly clean look.

A temporary stage had been erected in the city hall square and a rehearsal for a folk-dancing festival was taking place. To the accompaniment of an accordion and under the direction of a temperamentally gesticulating instructor, 'teen-aged boys and girls were practicing intricate Polish folk-dances. Taking photographs, I found myself surrounded by a group of young men who were speaking German and making depreciatory remarks about the dancers. I learned that some of them were Upper Silesians, others Sudetengermans who lived in the area between Oppeln and the Czech frontier. The latter and their families had recently been repatriated from the Soviet Union. The young men had little positive to say about life in Poland. Several of them were no more than eighteen years old and could have no clear memories of life under German rule. I felt that some of their remarks were the opinions of their elders, which they repeated. They soon confirmed this.

"At home we never forget Germany," one of them said.

They did not want to join in public performances such as the dancing. "These things are organized for the Poles, but not for us," they said. All the houses on the "Marktplatz", the square around the city hall, had recently been rebuilt, they told me, but, in line with their generally negative attitude, did not have anything good to say about this work. "They are hardly finished before everything starts to collapse again," one lad remarked and the others agreed with him.

The choice of goods in the shops of Oppeln reminded of Warsaw and Gdynia. As everywhere else, there was no lack of drunken men here, but the general impression of Oppeln was that of a comparatively prosperous and well-kept community.

Before reaching *Gross-Strehlitz*, we stopped once more and photographed a farm house. The owners came out and talked to us. They were Germans, an elderly couple and their son,—a young man with one arm, who until recently had been a prisoner-of-war in Russia. While other Germans in this eastern district had never hesitated to speak their language, and, if they felt so inclined, to complain about their lot, these three people were timid and uneasy.

"It's best to say nothing and to work and go on living," the young man murmured. "We have gone through enough. Now we beg only to have peace."

In Gross-Strehlitz, which is now called Strzelce Opol, the brief respite from war-scars, ruins and filth was over. The town looked as depressing as most others west of Oppeln. A young man came to talk to us while we were stopped at a gasoline pump. He told us he was an Upper Silesian Pole who had been in the German forces during the war and spent some years as a prisoner-of-war in the United States. He was very bitter and said he would give anything to be able to return to North America. He whispered this as he stood at the window of the car, adding:

"The people standing around here only pretend to admire your car. But I tell you, everyone listens, trying to find out who says what to whom. We have no freedom. The stalinist dictatorship is over, but instead we have another kind."

We drove on, through *Peiskretscham* (Pyskowice) and entered the Upper Silesian industrial district. Soon we saw the first great factories, blast-furnaces and steel mills which justly gave this part of Silesia the name "the East-German Ruhr". Then began the countless rows of workers' flats and minutes later we entered the city of *Gleiwitz*, now Gliwice. Here was another industrial city which escaped wartime destruction. What damage there may have been has long been repaired,—particularly, of course, among the buildings of the heavy industries and the coal mines.

It was immediately clear that the industries are operating at full capacity. The city is anything but beautiful, but because of the industrial activity it does not seem nearly as gloomy as most others we have visited on this journey. The town may be more neglected and dirtier than before, and there is certainly less traffic than in pre-war days; the state-shops look bare, (although they are well supplied with goods by comparison with other polish cities) and the people are poorly dressed. But despite this, smoke billows from the factory

269

chimneys, the mine elevators rumble into the depths of the earth, the factory halls hum day and night and the freight trains puff in and out of the yards at short intervals.

The industrial towns in this area practically overlap. Thus we did not notice when we left Gleiwitz and entered Hindenburg,—now called Zabrze. Once we realized we had reached the latter town, we also found that its condition resembled that of Gleiwitz in every way. Shortly after *Hindenburg,* almost exactly at the location of the pre-1939 German-Polish border, we were once more stopped by a police patrol. A young militiaman glanced at our documents and explained in fluent German, that most control points were intended for a check-up of driver's lincenses: so many Poles were driving state vehicles without permits and without official approval, he said; then followed a lenghthy conversation about our car and its technical data. Finally the officer thanked me for the information I had given him and saluted.

"Have a good trip with your green giant of a car!" he called after us. The green giant of a car rolled on and we left the former German territories under Polish administration.

LAST NOTES IN THE DIARY

The scene before our eyes during the past weeks was always sad, almost constantly gloomy, and in a large measure hopeless; sometimes it had moments of tragic-comedy.

As reported by us, this scene will make an even more terrible impression on many people, particularly on the millions who have lost their homes in this land. But we hope that we will not only evoke painfull feelings. After the many events which have irrevocably taken place, it would be a pity if logical reflections were to be made impossible by understandable, but nonetheless impulsive, emotional judgements.

It is true that towards the end of the war, statesmen gathered at international conferences, made decisions which the West today has reasons to regret. It is also true that those responsible for carrying out these decisions, in sofar as they affected the former German territories under Polish administration, acted harshly, in a radical and often brutal manner. Many people were made to suffer and others to lose their lives, who in frequent cases were the least responsible for the actions for which Germany was to be punished.

It is true that the former German territories are today in a condition which has to be seen to be believed,—and this in an age which we call civilized and in which millions of people have no roofs over their heads and insufficient bread to keep themselves alive.

Yes, all this is true.

But it is also true that at the time of the conferences, when the statesmen made their decisions, a war was being waged against an unyielding enemy who stopped at nothing; an enemy whose leader, whose "Führer", dit not hesitate to exploit occupied territories like Poland until they collapsed. An alliance between East and West which had been forced into existence by the enemy himself, had to be kept strong to wage this war. And the eastern partner of this alliance demanded high prices.

It is also true that the Poles who took over the former German territories had gone to a thorough school: they too had been driven out and deported, they knew from bitter experience how territories are occupied and how one exploits an area as quickly as possible without concern for the future.

It is also true that the retreating German armies contributed a great deal to the present condition of the former German territories under Polish administration: cities,—large and small,—were turned into "fortresses" and defended until nothing was left of them. Many could surely have been spared.

None of these truths on either side of this historical profit-and-loss account cancels out or equalizes the other. No final balance sheet can ever be drawn up. But perhaps the situation permits a few realistic conclusions:

It is hopeless to speak of rights and justice in a question such as this, as long as the great powers of the world dance around each other like boxers ready to strike at any moment. At such a time claims of rights and demands for justice by smaller nations are only exploited by the great powers for propaganda purposes. But that is not all. Many other manoeuvers belong to the prancing and dancing, shifting and weaving of the great powers: these include the creation of protective buffer-states and the moving of an entire nation several longitudinal degrees to the west.

No, in this sad epoch of the world's history, rights are rarely respected and real justice is almost never meted out.

No one is very much concerned over the fact that East Prussia, eastern Pomerania, East Brandenburg and Silesia were settled by Germans during centuries. Once upon a time this was the primitive frontier-land of western culture. With some exceptions it was the Germans who brought culture and civilization to this frontier. Today the same land is sinking back into its original primitive condition. This desintegration is far advanced.

Whatever may be the future of these territories,—it is at least to be hoped that continuing peace and growing human insight will help to end the sadness, the gloom and the hopelessness. May the people who live there, be they Germans or Poles, be granted an existance worthy of the civilized christian world.

E N D

GRÜNBERG. Like Köslin and Allenstein, Grünberg is a provincial capital and, like the other two, has become more important under the polish administration than it was in german times. We saw few signs of wartime damage here and the town made a lively impression —— a pleasant change.

In Grünberg as everywhere else, a large crowd gathered whenever we stopped. While Jacqueline bought some supplies, I took this picture of the people admiring our car.

CHRISTIANSTADT. It was astonishing how little interest the polish authorities displayed in rebuilding former german industries. A typical example: the huge and only slightly damaged I. G. Farben chemical trust's factories and houses in Christianstadt. Everything stood empty.

SAGAN. The picture above shows the neglected ducal chateau in Sagan. In the equally neglected park of the chateau we saw Russians walking about, clad in pyjamas. Below: a partial view of the monastery in Sagan. It contains, according to a polish citizen of the town, »the oldest astronomical observatory in Poland«.

SCHWEIDNITZ. [In]
this small silesian tow[n]
we met one of the tw[o]
last german protesta[nt]
pastors who still wor[k]
ed in the territories und[er]
polish administration.

Upper left: pastor H[er]
bert Rutz and Fr[au]
Rutz in their flat.
Lower left: the Pea[ce]
Church, the church [of]
the german protesta[nt]
parish of Schweidni[tz.]
Pastor Rutz looked af[ter]
19 rests of parishes wi[th]
a total of 2,000 p[a]
rishioners.
Right: An incura[bly]
injured foot made t[he]
pastor's task even mo[re]
difficult. Here he u[ses]
two crutches to walk [to]
his church.

Upper left: proof that the worst time of persecution is over for the Germans in this area, is this sign in Polish and German at the entrance of the church in Schweidnitz.

Upper right: these are the last german hymn books left to the ever-dwindling parish in Schweidnitz.

Lower right: when Pastor Rutz went further afield, he only used a single cane, not wishing to attract too much attention to his sick foot. Thus he worsened his condition. He owned no means of transportation, depended on busses and trains and the occasional opportunity to hitch-hike when visiting his 19 parishes.

We drove pastor Rutz to the nearby town of Reichenbach where he supervised pre-confirmational instruction. This class began with 18 pupils. Only two boys and two girls remained at the time of our visit. The others had all emigrated with their parents (above).

Pastor and Frau Rutz with their thirteen year old daughter Eveline. The girl was learning to play the organ in order to be able to help out at her father's church. (lower left).

On our return from the former german territories under polish administration we received the stunning news that pastor Rutz had died. His death was a great loss —— not only for his family, but for the remaining members of his nineteen parishes.

Poland is overwhelmingly roman catholic. Since the advent of the Gomulka administration, attendance at churches has greatly increased. During services churches
are frequently filled to overflowing and many worshipers have to remain outside.

In the south west silesian mountains, the »Riesengebirge«, we visited the village of
Agnetendorf, and after some searching, found the villa which belonged to the late
german dramatist Gerhart Hauptmann. The house has been renovated recently
and is being used as a children's home.

HIRSCHBERG. The market square (»Marktplatz«) looks as if battles had been fought here. Yet, there was no fighting in Hirschberg nor was the city bombed. These baroque buildings on one side of the square have collapsed due to neglect. Some reconstruction has been begun but much remains to be done.

On one side of the market square in Hirschberg the houses are well kept.

BRESLAU. In the center of Breslau a good deal of construction is going on. On the »Ring« — the streets around the city hall — the rebuilding programme is almost completed. The city hall, seen in this picture, has been refurbished. In the foreground a private car, recognizable by the letter »H« on its license plate.

Many parts of Breslau, both in the suburbs and in the center, still look exactly as they did at the end of the war. The area around a square once called the »Neumarkt«, located in the heart of the city, is one example.

At other places, as for instance along a main street once called the »Schuhbrücke«, new blocks of flats are being built. This is also in the center of the town.

The street leading towards the Breslau Cathedral was a total loss, but has been rebuilt (above). With the help of a prewar picture (left) we noticed that when reconstructed, the buildings were not placed the same way, even though they have been faithfully copied. The top parts of the cathedral's steeples are still missing.

On the edge of the destroyed »Neumarkt« square, I came across this group of »private businessmen«: invalids who were selling light bulbs, razor blades, pencils and the like. They were a cheerful and friendly lot.

Elsewhere on the »Neumarkt« private business was also transacted: private farmers, increasing in numbers since the Gomulka administration and recently freed form many restrictions, were selling fruits and vegetables.

The Elizabeth Church in Breslau is one of the landmarks which have been restored.
It had only been slightly damaged in the war.

This side of the »Ring« around the Breslau city hall was still greatly disfigured when we visited the town in 1956. Now all buildings but one are completed and the last will soon be ready.

The chief hotel for foreigners in Breslau is the »Monopol«. It is badly run but always full, particularly in summer, when bus-tours stop here.

The Elizabeth Church in Breslau is one of the landmarks which have been restored. It had only been slightly damaged in the war.

This side of the »Ring« around the Breslau city hall was still greatly disfigured when we visited the town in 1956. Now all buildings but one are completed and the last will soon be ready.

The chief hotel for foreigners in Breslau is the »Monopol«. It is badly run but always full, particularly in summer, when bus-tours stop here.

LIEGNITZ. The headquarters of the russian Warsaw Pact Forces are located here. Though grossly neglected, some historical buildings, such as the famed »Gabeljürge« fountain and near-by town houses, are still standing. The lower picture, taken before the war, indicates to what extent neglect has already caused the buildings to crumble (see above).

LÜBEN. The former »Ring« of this town is in shambles. Only one building has been reconstructed and is used as a city hall. Since the house has the same arcades as its predecessor, I was able to make the photograph above from the identical position as the one below, which was taken twenty years earlier. The comparison is shocking.

While I was photographing in Lüben these men came to watch me. They would have fitted into any eastern polish or russian village.

Between Lüben and Glogau we came across this inn. The building seemed to be a symbol: the german writing on it was faded but still legible, the polish sign was already broken and looked shabbier than the original inscription.

GLOGAU. I stood on heaps of rubble overgrown with weeds and grass and photographed these dreadful ruins. As far as the eye could see, only grotesque shapes stood where once had been a beautiful city sheltering 30,000 people.

Again a comparison: the massive steeple of the parish church of Glogau has been reduced to a stump. The second steeple appearing in the background, below, has vanished. The building on the right, above, now serves as an emergency church.

Between Glogau and Steinau we passed this state farm, recognizable by the sign »P. G. R.« (above). The buildings were in a state of disrepair, many fields were fallow. The central yard of the large farm looked like a trash dump (below).

Some of the «P. G. R.« workers (above) came to us and
were pleased to be photo-
graphed. Among them a wo-
man and her child (below).
Note the writing on the wall
in the background.

Near Steinau we saw numerous farm houses which looked very ill-kept. The house above was no exception. The windows filled in with bricks indicate that these are easier to obtain then glass.

STEINAU. The small town showed many scars of war and was dirty. Only the russian war memorial and the square around it looked comparatively clean.

NIMPTSCH. We passed this town on our way from Breslau to Upper Silesia and were glad to note that there were no ruins to be seen.

FRANKENSTEIN, in southern Silesia, had also suffered little damage. When we stopped on the market square the usual crowd had soon gathered.

KAMENZ. The castle which belonged to a branch of the german Kaiser's family was severely damaged during the war, but the church below was well preserved.

PATSCHKAU. We tried to drive through the main street of this little town but it was blocked. A man told us that houses on both sides of the street were expected to collapse.

NEISSE. The upper picture shows the famous »Schöne Brunnen« — or »beautiful fountain« — as it looked before the war. Using the tower in the background as a means of reference, I could pinpoint the spot where the fountain must have stood. All that is left is a piece of pipe sticking out of the ground, — undoubtedly the fountain's water supply.

The well-known »Kämmereigebäude« in Neisse (above), once considered the finest late-renaissance structure in Silesia, is one of the few architectural landmarks which has been rebuilt. Decorations and murals are still missing but may be added later. The almost completely destroyed Jakobi Church (below) may also be rebuilt some day. A scaffolding had been erected over its nave.

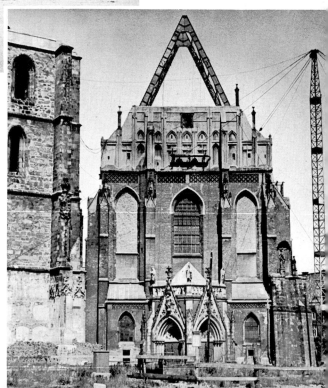

OPPELN. The city hall of this Upper Silesian town built in pseudo-italian style, has been renovated, contributing to the well-kept and neat look of the town's center.

Before the city hall of Oppeln a temporary stage had been erected and on it young men and women were rehearsing for a folk-dancing festival (above). Among those watching the rehearsal were several lads of german origin who made sarcastic remarks about the dancing and the recently rebuild houses on the square (below). The latter were no sooner finished than they collapsed again, the lads claimed.

In the area around Oppeln we saw numerous well-kept farm houses in neat gardens (above). The surrounding fields were in good condition (below). We were able to establish that the owners were usually Germans. These were people with strong ties to the soil but also with a sound knowledge of polish, — — traditional in Upper Silesia, and helpful when dealing with the authorities.

GROSS STREHLITZ. In this town the brief respite from damage and destruction, which had begun west of Oppeln was over. The place looked like many other communities we had seen during the previous weeks.

GLEIWITZ, in the heart of Upper Silesia's industrial area, is by no means beautiful, but it does make as cheerless an impression as most other towns in the former German east. Its heavy industry saved it from total destruction.

Dirty, thin and poorly dressed children (above) and drunken men (below) were the order of the day during our journey. Poverty has led many people to seek escape in alcohol. The man below had just left the liquor shop in the background and was in an advanced state of inebriation. But he still knew enough to hide his face when I appeared.

HINDENBURG. Upper Silesia's heavy industry was active day and night. This was our last view of the former german territories under polish administration, as we crossed the pre-1939 German-Polish frontier. The total impression gained on our journey had been one of gloom and hopelessness, yet here was one decidedly positive aspect: work was going on, an effort was being made to alleviate Poland's ever-growing economic crisis.